VOLUME V ◆ NUMBER 2

SIGNIFICANT ISSUES ◆ SERIES

Northeast Asia in the 1980s
Challenge and Opportunity

Proceedings of a Conference
Sponsored by

The Georgetown Center for Strategic
& International Studies

and

The Institute of Foreign Affairs &
National Security, Seoul, Korea

July 28-29, 1982
Washington, D.C.

Robert L. Downen, Editor

Center for Strategic & International Studies
Georgetown University • Washington, D.C.

SIGNIFICANT ISSUES SERIES papers are written for and published by The Center for Strategic and International Studies, Georgetown University. The views expressed in these papers are those of the authors and not necessarily those of the Center.

Series Editor: Amos A. Jordan
Managing Editor: Jean C. Newsom

Center for Strategic and International Studies
Georgetown University
1800 K Street, N.W., Suite 400
Washington, D.C. 20006
(202) 887-0200

SIGNIFICANT ISSUES ◆ SERIES

NORTHEAST ASIA IN THE 1980s: CHALLENGE AND OPPORTUNITY

Proceedings of a Conference
Sponsored By

The Georgetown Center for Strategic
and International Studies

and

The Institute of Foreign Affairs and
National Security, Seoul, Korea

July 28-29, 1982
Washington, D.C.

Robert L. Downen, editor

Library of Congress Cataloging in Publication Data
Main entry under title:

Northeast Asia in the 1980s.

(Significant issues series, ISSN 0736-7163 ; v. 5, no. 2)
Proceedings of the Conference on "Northeast Asia in the 1980s: Challenge and Opportunity."
  1. East Asia—Strategic aspects—Congresses.
I. Downen, Robert L. II. Georgetown University. Center for Strategic and International Studies.
III. Oegyo Anbo Yŏn'guwŏn (Korea) IV. Conference on "Northeast Asia in the 1980s: Challenge and Opportunity" (1982: Washington, D.C.) V. Series: Significant issues series ; v. 5, no. 2.
UA830.N67   1983   355'.03305   83-5492

ISBN 0-89206-043-3
ISSN 0736-7163

UA 830 .N67 1983

Northeast Asia in the 1980s

UA 830 .N67 1983

Northeast Asia in the 1980s

UA
830
.N67
1983

© 1983
by
Center for Strategic & International Studies
Georgetown University ● Washington, D.C.

All Rights Reserved

Contents

Preface	v
Participants	vi
I. Opening Remarks	1
• Dr. Ray S. Cline	3
• Dr. Amos A. Jordan	6
• The Honorable Young-Choo Kim	7
• The Honorable Jong Chan Lee	8
• The Honorable S.I. Hayakawa	12
II. The Power Constellation in Northeast Asia	17
1. The Defense of Korea, by Edward Luttwak and Steven L. Canby	19
2. Japanese Security Responsibility: Korean Perspectives, by Bae-Ho Hahn	39
3. Japanese Security Responsibility, by Michael Blaker	46
4. Antihegemonism and U.S.-PRC-Japanese Security Cooperation, by Dal Choong Kim	51
5. The Sino-Soviet Conflict and its Impact on the Korean Peninsula, by Chang-Yoon Choi	56
6. Sino-Soviet Relations in the 1980s as a Factor in Northeast Asian Security, by Thomas W. Robinson	64
III. Two Koreas in a Changing Environment	71
7. Political Succession in North Korea, by Suk-Ryul Yu	73
8. North Korea after Kim Il-sung, by Ralph Clough	81
9. The Outlook of the Fifth Republic of Korea: A Study of the Socialization Process of the New Political Leaders, by Brigadier General Tong Hui Lee	87
10. Outlook for the Fifth Republic in the 1980s: International Law Implications of "Economic Diplomacy," by Nam-Yearl Chai	92
11. Two Koreas in the Global Context, by Kie-Pyung Oh	95
12. Changing Environment and the Two Koreas in the 1980s, by Seung Hwan Kim	101

IV.	Agenda for U.S.-Korean Cooperation in the 1980s	109
	13. ROK-U.S. Military Alliance in the 1980s, by Yong-ok Park	111
	14. U.S.-ROK Security in the 1980s: The U.S. Role, by William J. Taylor	116
	15. U.S.-Korean Security Cooperation: South Korea's Security Role, by Yu-Nam Kim	122
	16. South Korea's Security Role in the Current Decade, by Larry Niksch	129
	17. Prospects for Broadening U.S.-Korean Cooperation, by Young Nok Koo	134
	18. Whales and Fishes: The Future of U.S.-Korean Cooperation, by Donald Macdonald	140
V.	Conclusions: Principal Issues and Policy Implications	147
	19. Security and Strategy in Northeast Asia: A Korean View, by Young-Choo Kim	149
VI.	Closing Remarks	157
	• Dr. Ray S. Cline	159
	• Ambassador Young-Choo Kim	163
	• The Honorable Duwan Pong	164
	Appendix	166
	About the Editor	169

PREFACE

In July of 1982, the Pacific Basin Project of the Georgetown University Center for Strategic and International Studies, in conjunction with the Institute of Foreign Affairs and National Security of the Republic of Korea, held a conference in Washington, D.C. to examine future prospects for the Northeast Asian region. For two days, some 40 American and Korean conference delegates—all noted specialists in Asian-Pacific strategic affairs—discussed a variety of opportunities and challenges likely to confront the nations of the area during the 1980s.

Not all projections were positive. With the global recession's current impact on the economies of the region, the prospect of imminent leadership successions in Moscow and Pyongyang, and an uncertain power balance on the Korean peninsula in the coming years, most of the conferees agreed that serious trials lie ahead for the Republic of Korea, the United States, and for regional peace and stability in general. Nevertheless, the basic consensus reached by the conferees and passed on to the observers in the audience seemed to be this: the determination of the South Korean people, coupled with strong and decisive U.S. commitment and an appropriate degree of assistance from Japan, should be equal to any threat or challenge that is posed to Northeast Asia over the coming decade. The scholarly analysis behind this conclusion is reflected in the following summary of papers presented at the conference, and it should be valuable reading for academicians and policy practitioners alike.

I would like to thank Philip Fahy for his help as rapporteur and as editor, and JoAnn Walters and Stephanie Clipper for their help in preparing this manuscript for publication.

Robert L. Downen
Director
Pacific Basin Project
January 1983

VISITING DELEGATION
Republic of Korea

Hon. Young-Choo Kim
Head of Delegation
Institute of Foreign
 Affairs and National Security

Hon. Jong Chan Lee
National Assembly

Hon. Chung Soo Park
National Assembly

Hon. Joong Yeon Cho
National Assembly

Hon. Duwan Pong and Mrs. Pong
National Assembly

Hon. Churl Soon Yim
National Assembly

Jong Heup Park
National Assembly

Yu Nam Kim
Institute of Foreign
 Affairs and National Security

Suk Ryul Yu
Institute of Foreign
 Affairs and National Security

Young Choi
Institute of Foreign
 Affairs and National Security

Kuk Chin Kim
Institute of Foreign
 Affairs and National Security

Dae Yeol Ku
Institute of Foreign
 Affairs and National Security

Ok Yul Kim
Sook Myung Women's University

Won Sul Lee
Kyung Hee University

Hai Hyung Cho
Kookmin University

Bae Ho Han
Korea University

Dal Choong Kim
Yonsei University

Tong Hui Lee
Korean Military Academy

Kie Pyung Oh
Sogang University

Young Nok Koo
Seoul National University

Yong Ok Park
National Defense College

Eun Taik Lee
Samsung Shipbuilding Co., Ltd.

Choong Kun Cho
Hanil Development Co., Ltd.

Duck Choong Kim
Daewoo Corporation

Hoon Yang
Hyundai Co., Ltd.

Wuk Rai Cho
Hyosung Aluminium Co., Ltd.

Bong Hyuk Kay
Korean Traders Association

Byung Chul Seo
Institute of Foreign
 Affairs and National Security

LOCAL PARTICIPANTS

John Alison
Northrop Corporation

Dora Alves
CSIS

James Auer
U.S. Department of Defense

William Barnds
Office of Congressman
Stephen Solarz

John Bernard
CSIS

Michael Blaker
CSIS

Allan Bloom
Vought Corporation

William Breer
U.S. Department of State

Leslie Burgess
IBM

Jong Kyou Byun
Embassy of Korea

Steven L. Canby
C&L Associates

Ann Campagna
CSIS

Nam-Yearl Chai
Columbus College

Sun-Eui Choi
Embassy of Korea

Marjorie Cline
CSIS

Ray S. Cline
CSIS

Stephanie Clipper
CSIS

Ralph Clough
The Washington Center of
  the Asia Society

Frank Davenport
U.S. Department of State

Robert L. Downen
CSIS

Philip Fahy
CSIS

Carl Ford
Office of Senator John Glenn

Jeffrey Gayner
The Heritage Foundation

Ralph Greenhouse
U.S. ICA

David Gries
U.S. Government

Guy Hicks
DIA

Paul Holman
DIA

Amos A. Jordan, Jr.
CSIS

Stanton Jue
U.S. ICA

Chong-Nak Kim
Embassy of Korea

J.C. Kim
Embassy of Korea

Seung Hwan Kim
CSIS

Suk-han Kim
Arnold & Porter

Young C. Kim
George Washington University

Han-Choon Lee
Embassy of Korea

Herbert Lee
U.S. ICA

Suck-ho Lee
George Washington University

Ted Lewis
CSIS

Koo Chang Lim
Embassy of Korea

Edward Luttwak
CSIS

Donald Macdonald
U.S. Department of State

Robert Magner
U.S. Government

Bob Martin
U.S. Department of Defense

Byung Suk Min
Embassy of Korea

Michael Moodie
CSIS

Ronald Morse
The Woodrow Wilson Center

Larry Niksch
Congressional Research Service

Hisahiko Okazaki
CSIS

Chong-Sang Park
Embassy of Korea

Mary B. Park
CSIS

Yun Park
Embassy of Korea

John Parker
Mobil Oil Corporation

William Pittman
CSIS

David Reese
U.S. Government

Charles Richardson
Martin Marietta

Thomas W. Robinson
Georgetown University

Chang Hee Roe
Embassy of Korea

Gaston Sigur
National Security Council

William Scully
The Heritage Foundation

Jang-nai Sohn
Embassy of Korea

Robert Sutter
Congressional Research Service

Bruce Swanson
Lockheed-Georgia Company

Akira Takata
CSIS

Seiji Tanaka
Fuji Telecasting Co., Ltd.

William J. Taylor
CSIS

Keiichi Torii
Fuji Telecasting Co., Ltd.

M. Jon Vondracek
CSIS

Gregory F.T. Winn
U.S. ICA

Herman Witthaus
General Motors Corporation

Kwan-Ha Yim
Manhattanville College

Dr. Ray S. Cline, CSIS, opens the Conference on July 28, 1982. Looking on are National Assemblymen Churl Soon Yim, Duwan Pong, Joong Yeon Cho, Chung Soo Park, and Jong Chan Lee; Ambassador Young-Choo Kim, IFANS; Amos Jordan, CSIS; Jang-nai Sohn, Embassy of Korea; and Ok Yul Kim, Sook Myung Women's University.

Breakfast session with Senator John Glenn on July 30, 1982. He is flanked by the Majority Leader of the Korean National Assembly, Jong Chan Lee (left), and by Korean Ambassador to the United States, Byong Hion Lew (right).

Korean Delegation Leader Young-Choo Kim of IFANS (left) greets U.S. Assistant Secretary of State for East Asia John Holdridge (right), as Dr. Ray Cline looks on.

At the July 29, 1982 Decatur House reception for Korean visitors, Secretary of the United States Army John O. Marsh, Jr. (center), talks with Deputy Director of Politico-Military Affairs at the State Department, Stefan Halper, Korean Assemblymen Chung Soo Park and Jong Chan Lee; and Jang-nai Sohn of the Embassy of Korea.

Dr. Ray Cline, Senior Associate at CSIS (center), chats with Korean Ambassador to the United States Byong Hion Lew (left) and Jang-nai Sohn of the Embassy of Korea, at the July 29 reception.

United States Congressman David R. Bowen of Mississippi (right), visits with Korean Ambassador Lew, National Assemblyman Duwan Pong, and Dr. Cline.

On July 27, United States Senator S.I. Hayakawa, Chairman of the Senate Foreign Relations Subcommittee on East Asia and the Pacific, escorted Korean National Assemblymen to the Senate Chambers. From left: Churl Soon Yim, Joong Yeon Cho, Jong Chan Lee, Hayakawa, Chung Soo Park, and Duwan Pong.

Congressional Record

United States of America

PROCEEDINGS AND DEBATES OF THE 97th CONGRESS, SECOND SESSION

Vol. 128   WASHINGTON, TUESDAY, JULY 27, 1982   No. 99

Senate

VISIT TO THE SENATE BY A DELEGATION OF PARLIAMENTARIANS FROM THE REPUBLIC OF KOREA

Mr. HAYAKAWA. Mr. President, it is my pleasure to present the distinguished delegation of Parliamentarians from the Republic of Korea: The Honorable Jong Chan Lee, the floor leader or the majority leader of the Democratic Justice Party; the Honorable Chung Soo Park, an independent; the Honorable Joong Yeon Cho, senior whip of the opposition party; the Honorable Duwan Pong, an independent; and the Honorable Churl Soon Yim, a member of the Democratic Justice Party and also of the Foreign Affairs Committee.

They are visiting our Nation's Capital on the occasion of the 100th anniversary of the Korean-American Friendship Treaty.

A 2-day conference organized by the Center for Strategic and International Studies will highlight the delegation's week long visit to Washington. Their visit during this centennial year of the establishment of diplomatic relations between our two countries is another example of the cooperation and mutual understanding that exists between us. I look forward to our continuing friendship during the next 100 years and we welcome them.

I

Opening Remarks

Dr. Ray S. Cline, Senior Associate, CSIS; Leader of the U.S. Delegation

Good morning, ladies and gentlemen. I am Ray Cline, a senior associate of the Center for Strategic and International Studies (CSIS), of Georgetown University, and I have the great honor to be the leader of the U.S. delegation of experts on Northeast Asia who are meeting today in conference with a very distinguished delegation from the Republic of Korea. The topic of our discussion for the next two days is, "Northeast Asia in the 1980s: Challenge and Opportunity."

I am told by my friends who know the Chinese language that there are two component characters making up the single character for the word "crisis," one meaning "danger" or "challenge," the other "opportunity." I believe this is a very appropriate term for our conference because we are all aware of real strategic and security dangers in the Northeast Asian area and the Northwest Pacific area, but we feel that through common understanding, consultation, and cooperation with friends like those from the Republic of Korea, the United States can join with its allies in meeting these dangers and taking advantage of the opportunities.

The Honorable Clement J. Zablocki, chairman of the Foreign Affairs Committee of the United States House of Representatives, agreed to be the chairman of this conference. He has followed our preparations with great interest. We have exchanged correspondence many times.

Yesterday, Chairman Zablocki told me, as I know full well, that our Congress is in emergency session on a number of important pieces of legislation, most particularly the federal budget, and the voting of appropriations for our military program next year. This is a very controversial matter. We are talking about $180 billion, if I remember, and our Congress is meeting day and night.

Congressman Zablocki asked me to say that he had tried to make arrangements to be here to greet you, but he is being obliged to chair two different committee hearings this morning. He'll be shuttling back and forth between two committee rooms, and in that situation he was unable to come. He did send me, just this morning, a note which I would like to present in greeting you on his behalf.

Fortunately, the cochairman of this conference, a distinguished member of the Korean Diet, Mr. Jong Chan Lee, has kindly consented to accept the heavy responsibility of being the principle conference chairman, who will keep us all in line during these two days on behalf of Congressman Zablocki as well as himself.

CLEMENT J. ZABLOCKI
4TH DISTRICT, WISCONSIN

CHAIRMAN
COMMITTEE ON
FOREIGN AFFAIRS

Congress of the United States
House of Representatives
Washington, D.C. 20515

July 28, 1982

Dr. Ray S. Cline
Senior Associate
The Center for Strategic & International Studies
1800 K Street
Washington, D.C. 20006

Dear Dr. Cline:

The invitation to participate in the Conference on Northeast Asia in the 1980s is a distinct honor. Only the pressing legislative schedule of the United States Congress has prevented me from attending with you today and actively engaging in the sessions which are devoted to timely and significant considerations.

The two days you are about to commit to intense discussion are particularly appropriate this year which marks the one-hundredth anniversary of the establishment of diplomatic relations between the United States and Korea. The joint sponsorship and active participation of two highly respected academic institutions, one in Washington, D.C. and the other in Seoul, exemplify how well bilateral U.S.-Korean relations have prospered. During the past 100 years, these relations have included extensive educational exchange of benefit to both nations. Therefore, the meeting today and tomorrow follows a great tradition and should add a new dimension to the intellectual interaction between our two peoples.

I send my greetings to all the participants, to the Korean and American scholars and officials, but in particular to the several foreign guests that have traveled the long way across the Pacific Ocean to attend. I wish you great success in your quest for understanding and direction on the important issues we face together in the coming years in the Northeast Asian region.

Sincerely yours,

CLEMENT J. ZABLOCKI
Member of Congress

CJZ:vpj

I would like to say that we are flattered and honored to have such a large and distinguished delegation from Korea. It is very impressive, and I would like to welcome the leader of the Korean delegation, Ambassador Young-Choo Kim, who is a very distinguished member of the foreign service of the Republic of Korea and now acting chancellor of the sponsoring organization in Korea, the Institute of Foreign Affairs and National Security (IFANS), and ask him to introduce us to the Korean delegation so that we can all recognize the speakers.

Ambassador Young-Choo Kim: We would like to extend our personal greetings to our American friends, so may I ask each member of the Korean delegation to introduce himself:

> Tong Hui Lee, Dean of the Academic Board of the Korean Military Academy
> Young Nok Koo, Seoul National University
> Yong Ok Park, National Defense College
> Eun Taik Lee, Samsung Shipbuilding Co., Ltd.
> Choong Kun Cho, Korean Airlines
> Duck Choong Kim, Daewoo Cooperation
> Hoon Yang, Hyundai Corporation
> Wuk Rai Cho, Hyosung Aluminum Co., Ltd.
> Dal Choong Kim, Yonsei University
> Bae Ho Hahn, Korea University
> Hai Hyung Cho, Chairman of the Board, Kookmin University Foundation
> Bong Hyuk Kay, Korean Traders Association
> Yu Nam Kim, Institute of Foreign Affairs and National Security
> Won Sul Lee, Vice Chairman of Kyung Hee University
> Kie Pyung Oh, Sogang University
> Dae Yeol Ku, Institute of Foreign Affairs and National Security
> Kuk Chin Kim, Institute of Foreign Affairs and National Security
> Young Choi, Institute of Foreign Affairs and National Security
> Suk Ryul Yu, Institute of Foreign Affairs and National Security
> Ok Yul Kim, Sook Myung Women's University
> Byung Chul Seo, Institute of Foreign Affairs and National Security

Dr. Cline: Thank you very much. We are also glad to have Minister Jang-nai Sohn here from the Embassy of the Republic of Korea, who has helped very much in facilitating communications to arrange for this conference between our two countries. We are especially gratified that we have such a fine turnout of representatives from the international business community in Korea, as well as distinguished members of Korean universities and the distinguished members of the National Assembly in Seoul.

I was speaking on the telephone this weekend with the chairman of our Center, David Abshire, whom I think many of our guests know and I think you know. He apologized to me profusely and asked me to apologize to you for his absence. He is not within 2,000 miles of the city of Washington; he is obliged to be in California, or

I am sure he would have been here this morning. He told me that Korea is very near and dear to his heart, because his first assignment after graduating from the U.S. Military Academy was to go to Korea and get shot at for awhile and to serve in a role that made him very familiar with the strategic importance of that country. Today he is in California on a prescheduled trip arranged even as we were arranging this conference, and we were not able to adjust the schedules. He asked me to welcome you on his behalf. In addition, he and I have agreed to request our vice chairman of CSIS, the chief operating officer of this research organization, Dr. Amos Jordan, to give you a formal greeting as representative of the Center.

Dr. Amos A. Jordan, Jr., Vice Chairman and Chief Operating Officer, CSIS

On behalf of the Georgetown Center for Strategic and International Studies, I want to welcome each of you to this "Conference on Northeast Asia in the 1980s: Challenge and Opportunity." Our Center is pleased to be host to this significant forum and to share in its sponsorship with the Institute of Foreign Affairs and National Security, of Seoul, Korea. I want to extend a special welcome to Assemblyman Jong Chan Lee, our conference chairman, and the leader of the Korean Delegation, Ambassador Young-Choo Kim, as well as all the members of the Korean National Assembly whom we are honored to have with us on this occasion. We are delighted to welcome such a distinguished group of conferees; your participation in this conference is testimony to the continuing strong ties between the peoples of our two countries.

We anticipate two days of extremely productive dialogue between the scholars of our two research institutions, which should open our eyes to the many challenges confronting the United States and South Korea in the decade ahead. We expect there to be strong attention given to the importance of regional cooperation, which has been a particular concern of our own Pacific Basin Project here at CSIS. Whether we are looking at the regional future from an economic, security, or social perspective, the importance of regular communication and cooperative planning among Pacific Basin nations cannot be overemphasized.

Three years ago, the Georgetown Center, under the auspices of the Pacific Basin Project and the Future of Business Project, held two separate conferences for American and Korean scholars and officials, concentrating on the outlook for Korean "prosperity and vulnerability" in the global marketplace and on the potential for further growth in U.S.-Korean business cooperation. Now, this year, we are hosting a major conference which will explore common security problems as well as the strategic balance in the Asian-Pacific region. Together, these forums reflect the continuing interest of CSIS in those matters affecting the future of relations between our two countries in particular and between the United States and the Asian-Pacific region more generally.

I wish you well in your undertakings during these two days, and trust you will enjoy your stay at CSIS and in Washington.

Dr. Cline: I want to introduce the leader of the Korean delegation, and ask him to make a few remarks. Ambassador Young-Choo Kim is a very distinguished member of the foreign service of his country. He has been vice minister of foreign affairs; his most recent foreign post was ambassador to Austria; and in 1980 he was appointed chief of the delegation at Panmunjom for talks with the North Koreans on proposals for a meeting of prime ministers. He tells me somehow the telephone system in North Korea doesn't seem to work very well. The North Koreans haven't got the message. We're very delighted to have Ambassador Kim as the leader of this delegation and hope he is willing to express his sentiments at this time.

Ambassador Young-Choo Kim, IFANS Acting Chancellor; Leader of the Korean Delegation

Thank you very much, Dr. Jordan, for your kind words of welcome to our delegation. We all are very pleased to be here this morning to discuss Northeast Asia.

Distinguished Delegates, Ladies and Gentlemen:

Representing the Institute of Foreign Affairs and National Security, and, at the same time, on behalf of the Korean Delegation, I would like to express our deep appreciation to you, Dr. Jordan, Dr. Cline, and through you, to our host organization, The Center of Strategic and International Studies, which has done such splendid work to prepare this conference on Northeast Asia and to make thoughtful arrangements for the visiting delegates.

It was yesterday, July 27, that we marked the twenty-ninth anniversary of the Korean armistice. Since then, three decades of problems have passed by. We are in that period of uneasy peace. Our two countries never failed to demonstrate our bond of solidarity and a firm determination against the common threats and dangers we have been facing in our area.

But the world has been changing radically. Our region, Northeast

Asia, has been changing more rapidly in various ways. It may be said that we are still facing threats of the same nature, but in different forms and in different power constellations. Under these circumstances, it is of vital importance for us to redefine international environments where we are placed so that we may share right perceptions and work out the most effective measures to cope with any eventuality. No doubt it is our joint responsibility because we are "in the same boat."

It is our immediate task because the strategic reality surrounding us does not allow us to lose time. This is really a momentous agenda today for all of us. This morning we assemble here for this purpose. This should not be a once-and-for-all project, but should be a modest beginning for our continuous efforts. I am sure this meeting will produce a most fruitful outcome.

Now I have the honor and pleasure of introducing the Honorable Jong Chan Lee, a representative and the majority leader of the Korean National Assembly. We are very pleased to have his presence at this meeting in the capacity of cochairman of the conference, a role that he was willing to accept. I would like to ask you to join me in extending our hearty welcome and warm greetings to him. May I invite him to take the chair and to speak—the Honorable Jong Chan Lee, the cochairman of the conference.

Jong Chan Lee, Majority Leader of ROK National Assembly; Cochairman of the Symposium

Mr. Chairman, honorable members of the U.S. Congress and the Korean National Assembly, distinguished representatives from the U.S. government, scholars, business leaders, ladies and gentlemen:

As cochairman of the first annual Korean-U.S. symposium on security and strategy in Northeast Asia, it is indeed my honor and privilege to have this opportunity to share with you our mutual concern and interest in the given theme of this important conference. I feel that today's symposium will provide a significant opportunity for those assembled here to examine the entire Northeast Asian situation for the 1980s.

Following World War II and increasing tension between the West and East, the Communists attempted to expand their sphere of influence by military force, intervening in the affairs of many Asian nations unlike their activity in Western Europe. There are numerous examples, including the establishment of the People's Republic of China [PRC] as a result of internal conflict, the outbreak of the

Korean War, the Communist overthrow of Vietnam in the early 1970s, and the communization of the Indochinese peninsula.

In Europe, the attainment of political and social stability and economic prosperity as well as a military balance have combined to prevent war. This condition made it also possible to conduct various forms of negotiations between the two blocs.

In Asia, however, political instability, economic underdevelopment, and social disorder eventually brought on war and consequently encouraged expansionism by Communists in the region.

To put it another way, in Europe they realized that the values to be preserved by maintaining the peace were far too precious to risk destroying them by resorting to war. In Asia, however, wars occurred in most cases because of the vague expectation that war, although it causes ruin, might create many new values that would be more beneficial than those that already existed.

Since the latter part of the 1970s, however, the people of Asia gradually began to recognize that this was a misconception. In other words, it has been demonstrated that "such a society that is newly constructed after total destruction" could not, under any circumstances, guarantee human dignity, political equality, or economic progress, but would only result in endless oppression and the degradation of human life.

In concert with this deep awakening of the peoples in Asia, the economic development of Japan has given great incentive to the region. Stimulated by Japanese economic progress, the developing countries of Asia are making impressive progress with their own economic development plans.

As we emerge into the 1980s with the expectation that an era of competition will eventually replace that of war, Asian countries are seeking peaceful solutions to all problems. To attain these goals, however, several important conditions must be carefully recognized and met.

The first thing to be considered is that when one nation suffers the ravages of war, all neighboring nations are adversely affected, resulting in a general disturbance of order in the region. Consequently, each nation should assume responsibility for the protection of the entire region under a system that delegates an equal share of responsibility to each country.

Second, each nation must exert its utmost efforts to achieve prosperity through growing economic cooperation. Each must also develop its national economy and improve its standard of living. By successfully accomplishing this, they should all be able to prove to themselves that these actions will effectively deter war and lead to fair competition.

Third, the necessity for the United States to continue active assistance to deter any military aggression should be rightly pointed out. All available data show us that Soviet military capabilities have been expanded in the Far East during the 1970s, and this appears to be the most serious threat to our region. The Soviet Pacific Fleet alone, at 1.5 million tonnage, surpasses the United States 7th Fleet. Its strength is twice as much. Under these circumstances, it is inevitable that the deterrence of Soviet military power must depend, by a great deal, on U.S. nuclear weapons and conventional forces.

I believe that only when we successfully meet these requirements will a new regional order in Asia and the Pacific be established in harmony with the one being sought in the West, thus ultimately contributing to world peace.

Northeast Asia, in particular, is a key area in measuring the security of Asia and the Pacific region. Four great powers of the world, namely the United States, Japan, the People's Republic of China, and the Soviet Union, together with South and North Korea, maintain a perilous coexistence through a delicate interaction of forming triangular relations among themselves. Because of the precarious geopolitical situation, this region has such a built-in vulnerability that even small frictions may immediately cause overall disruption of the balance of power and lead to total destruction of the existing regional order. The Republic of Korea is located in this strategically important area.

At this point, I would like to dwell on the U.S. policies toward Northeast Asia. It seems to me that the U.S. policies in this region have not sufficiently reflected a regional defense concept covering the entire Asia-Pacific Area. They seem to rely to a large extent, on a strategic area defense concept focusing primarily on the security of Japan.

In regard to the Republic of Korea, it has been unfortunately true that the defense of Korea has been regarded, at least in concept, as subordinate to that of Japan, and this fact was well pointed out in the Nixon-Sato Joint Communique of 1969. This basic concept and approach of the United States made it possible for Japan to project even less than 1 percent of its GNP for its defense budget, while the Republic of Korea bears a heavy burden of sacrificing 6 percent of its GNP for its national defense.

In regard to these budget allotments, it is important to view the military tension on the Korean peninsula as a regional matter, thereby viewing North Korean provocation as a potential threat to the region as a whole.

Is it imaginable that the North Korean military power, which consumes more than 15 percent of the GNP and maintains a 700 thousand-man army is only for the purpose of its own defense? I have my doubts.

Is it conceivable that the so-called export of revolution through which North Korea trains the guerrillas and supplies arms to them would be stopped automatically once they complete the communization of the entire Korean peninsula? I would certainly answer no.

Although the perception that Korea is a dagger pointed at the heart of Japan prevails, it would be more appropriate to say that the Korean problem is a dagger pointed at the entire Asian and Pacific region.

To ease these prevailing tensions in Northeast Asia and to bring durable peace to our region, we Koreans are making all our efforts with particular emphasis on the following three points.

First, through successful implementation of a planned defense program, our military capability will not be second to that of the North Koreans in the 1980s.

Second, we look forward to seeing mainland China continue its moderate line and the present Kim Il-sung regime in North Korea replaced by a more rational one that may also follow a moderate line. Thus, hopefully, such a regime would sincerely agree with us on a peaceful solution to the problems on the Korean peninsula.

Third, we anticipate that the United States will certainly continue to remain a Pacific power and play a vital role in the region.

When we have a confirmation that these expectations have been fulfilled, we then can relax with the knowledge that the security of our region has been significantly solidified.

Our region of Northeast Asia is usually recognized as the "Far East" by Western Europe. We might point out that the same region is the "Near West" in relation to the United States. If we look at our relationship from this perspective, the United States might [have] a better defined global picture of the problems of the world.

I now wish to conclude my opening remarks by expressing my sincere hope that this symposium will greatly contribute to the exploring of our mutual needs, particularly enhancing security in Asia and the Pacific region. On behalf of my colleagues, I wish to express my special appreciation to the faculty members of this prestigeous Center for Strategic and International Studies and the participants from the Institute of Foreign Affairs and National Security of the Republic of Korea who worked very hard to make this symposium a successful one.

Dr. Cline: I want to thank our Conference Chairman Lee very sincerely for those perceptive remarks. It is the keynote introduction to all of the discussions we will now have. Before we turn to the presentation of papers, I want to carry out a duty that I reserve to myself, to introduce the other members of the parliamentary delegation from Korea.

May I introduce to you the other four members of the National Assembly. Of course, our Conference Chairman Jong Chan Lee is the majority floor leader of that assembly, but we also are fortunate to have with us Assemblymen Chung Soo Park and Joong Yeon Cho. Perhaps I should say that Chung Soo Park is the leader of the independent delegation. He is said by his colleagues to be the most independent of the independents. He is a very powerful leader. We are fortunate in having so many elements of the assembly represented here from the majority party also. Then we have Assemblymen Duwan Pong and Churl Soon Yim. We are very honored to have all of you here.

The Honorable S.I. Hayakawa, U.S. Senator from California

Ladies and gentlemen and friends from the United States and from Korea: Let me start by taking this opportunity to extend my welcome to the distingished visitors and guests from the Republic of Korea and to my counterpart from the National Assembly in Seoul. I extend the most cordial greetings and wish that their visit might strengthen the long tradition of friendship between the governments of our two great countries. May you have a most successful, productive conference with your counterparts here in the United States.

I want to congratulate and thank Dr. Ray Cline and Ambassador Young-Choo Kim for their fine efforts to compose this valuable two-day forum on the outlook for Northeast Asia in the 1980s. I also want to congratulate Ambassador Kim and his associates of the Institute of Foreign Affairs and National Security in Seoul for their instrumental role in planning and facilitating this significant meeting of scholars here in Washington. It is testimony to the long tradition of friendship and cooperation between the American people and the Korean people that a convocation such as this should proceed so smoothly.

I have been twice to Korea, first on the sad occasion of the funeral of the late President Park, and then, a little over a year later, on the happy occasion of the inauguration of President Chun. On the latter occasion, which was a happy occasion indeed, I attended the long, long procession, parade, and ceremony to mark the inauguration of the president, and I want to give you some impressions I had of that parade.

The first part of the parade was not an unfamiliar sight; that is, there were military bands, not totally dissimilar to American or European military bands, and not totally dissimilar to high school bands in the United States. They were very skillfull: they marched well; they played well; but there were no surprises there so far as I was concerned. It was the latter part of the parade that really startled and thrilled me very, very much.

As I understood the program, the latter part of the parade constituted villages or provinces of Korea that sent out their folk dancers, their comedians, their dramatizations of local legends, their folk costumes, and other manifestations of their local cultures. They had clowns; they had acrobats; they had quite unusual costumes such as I had never seen before because city people in Seoul don't dress that way. And the thing that I recall so clearly is the vividness of the colors. The greens were the most vivid greens I ever saw. The purples were the most purple I ever saw. The yellows, the reds, the pinks—all the colors were so vivid, and the clowns were so funny, and the dancers were so graceful, and the girls were so beautiful, and the costumes were so flowing and poetic. Everything about the folk culture of Korea, summed up in about three-quarters of a parade, gave me insight into Korea that I otherwise would not have had.

Also, taking advantage of the fact that I was there for the inauguration, I stayed three extra days to go to Pohan and visit the great steel works there. I've been to steel mills in the United States, in California, Gary, Indiana, in Pittsburgh. And these were marvelous in comparison. Beautiful steelworks in Pohan! I understand they are way ahead of those in Japan as well. Anyway, I just want to tell you how terribly impressed I was on that occasion. They told me that there were I don't know how many employees working there. There was this long, long stretch of machinery completely mechanized, and I didn't see any employees. I still want to know where all those thousands of employees were. They must have been hidden underground like gnomes. Anyway, I'm glad the place had employees, although I didn't succeed in finding any.

Also, I went to Kyongju to see the ancient tombs and the archeological findings there—the ancient tombs and the artificial hills under which they buried princes and kings and emperors in the old days. They all were of great interest to me. There is a very impressive one outside Uppsala in Sweden, which I've examined. There are some in Mexico, which I've examined. For the first time I saw one that had been excavated in Korea. Each time these burial mounds tried to say something about a culture, about the cohesion of the culture, about kingship, about royalty as a symbol of the unity of that culture; and a thousand years, 10 thousand years, 5 thousand years after that culture has died, that symbol remains. That, perhaps, is the significance of the pyramids, those pyramids in Egypt, those pyramids that you see in Mexico, the great burial mound I saw in Uppsala, the burial mounds I saw in Korea. They have a profound national significance in saying, "we are a culture. We do revere our rulers, and in revering our rulers, we assert ourselves as a society."

To see how this principle operates in one society after another and how the memorials of that society exist for a thousand, 2 thousand, 5 thousand years after that society is dead—that impressed me very, very much.

And so, I recall those things about Korea with a great deal of sentiment, but the one thing I recall about Korea almost with tears in my eyes was when I visited the DMZ [Demilitarized Zone]. I never have been in a war, myself. I've not been a soldier except in the Canadian militia between wars, so it was only a picnic. But at the DMZ, I felt myself 30 seconds away from a war, that any minute, 30 seconds from now, war could break out. And I realized then the terrible danger in which Korea stood, and that danger can break out any minute, 30 seconds from now, one minute from now, a day from now, a week for now—when, we don't know. But Korea is in perpetual danger until some resolution is made of the differences between North and South Korea, and one must not forget this. At the same time that Korea prospers along with Hong Kong and Taiwan and Singapore and Japan and all the great growing industrial nations of Asia, the new industrial nations, we mustn't forget that Korea itself remains perpetually in danger until that problem is solved.

It is an honor therefore, tonight, to extend to you my profoundly fraternal feelings toward the Republic of Korea, and to say to you that I share your concern for the future of your brave nation and to wish you happiness, success, and prosperity. But the happiness, success, and prosperity of Korea is intimately tied up with the happiness, success, and prosperity of all the Asian nations, including especially ASEAN, the Philippines, Indonesia, Malaysia, Singapore, Thailand, Japan, Taiwan, and the PRC. In a sense, they have a common fate.

The differences between Communism and non-Communism are serious, but ultimately they have to be overcome because Asia is an entity, and the Pacific region is an entity. Because there are not wars going on there right now, we in America worry about Poland, we worry about Lebanon, we worry about the Falkland Islands, we worry about Afghanistan, we worry about whatever is in the newspapers from day to day. From day to day we don't have that kind of news about Indonesia, about Thailand, about Singapore, about Korea, but the fact that these Asian nations, the Pacific nations, are not in the newspapers every day, there are additional reasons why we should pay attention to them. We have to think about what the future holds for them.

Not many people in the United States, however important the United States may be, realize that the trade between the United States and the nations of the Pacific exceeds the trade across the Atlantic Ocean from which most of our population come. Our Pacific trade is greater than our Atlantic trade. Just from the point of view of money, which is a very important thing to all of us, the Pacific is more important to us than the Atlantic, and in that sense, Korea, or Japan, or Taiwan is more important to us than France, or Italy, or England. And since the question of money does project into the future, all of us Americans must think of the fact that, although we are at this end of the United States an Atlantic nation, at my end of the United States, in California, we are a Pacific nation, and we are the most important part of the United States. I say this in all modesty, as you can see.

Well, it has been a great evening, Ladies and Gentlemen, and I'm glad to communicate to you my deepest feelings about the sense of fraternity I have with the Pacific nations. My father, who died a few years ago at the age of 91, in a curious way determined my career before I was born. He was the outstanding student in English in his high school in Japan, and, therefore, at about the age of 18 he came to the United States. Among the first things he did, besides working as a kitchen boy in a San Francisco home, was to translate English poetry in Japanese for the Japanese language newspapers in San Francisco. The fact that I ultimately got a Ph.D. in English literature was sort of predetermined by certain events in by father's life before he was even married. So I feel that my father's life and my mother's, too, prefigured my own destiny. Just as my father himself tried to bind East and West by his translations—Emerson, Ruskin, Longfellow, Shakespeare, etc.—into Japanese to bring the cultures together, I think that, in my position as United States senator, whether I will it or not, I've inherited the job he started. Therefore, I'm very, very proud to be here with you tonight to continue a tradition that my father started. Thank you very much.

Jong Chan Lee: First of all, I have to say thank you very much to Senator Hayakawa for his good remarks on Korea and the other Asian-Pacific countries. To Dr. Cline and Senator Hayakawa, on behalf of the Korean participants of the conference, I wish to express our gratitude to our hosts of this evening's dinner for the kind invitation extended to our delegation. I also would like to extend our sincere appreciation to all the American participants, particularly to our colleagues from the Center for Strategic and International Studies of Georgetown University, for their warm welcome.

Ladies and gentlemen, I am pleased that we have been able to organize this conference in which distinguished scholars and business leaders of our two countries can participate in the discussion of issues of mutual concern. I am particularly pleased that my fellow National Assembly members are also in attendance and can benefit from the frank and open exchange among the participants of this conference. I hope this conference will be the first of many meetings that will strengthen the bond that unites our peoples. Let me ask you to join me now in a toast to the everlasting cooperation and friendship of our two countries.

II

The Power Constellation in Northeast Asia

1

THE DEFENSE OF KOREA

Edward N. Luttwak, *Senior Fellow in Strategic Studies, CSIS,*
and
Steven L. Canby, *C & L Associates*

Three conditions define the problem of providing security against North Korea, one geographic and fixed, one volitive and circumstantial, and one political.

The geography is of course unfavorable: Seoul, which is the center of the Korean economy and indeed of national life in addition to being the political-administrative capital, is located within 30 miles of the DMZ; this condition rules out a defense based on phased withdrawal (and U.S. reinforcement), and indeed any kind of elastic defense, while allowing only a shallow space for a defense-in-depth.

The circumstantial condition not imposed by fundamental factors incapable of change is of course the asymmetry between the two armed forces that North and South respectively deploy; the poorer North deploys a rich man's army with much heavy equipment, while the richer South deploys a poor man's army, inferior in armor and artillery, both quantitatively and also qualitatively, at least on average. In part this reflects the different budgetary priorities of the two Koreas, one totalitarian and heavily militarized, while the other is primarily oriented toward economic development and social amelioration—notwithstanding its coups and governments of military background. But another important factor is the relatively greater investment that the South makes in its air and naval forces, even though the latter cannot in fact contribute significantly to the immediate defense of the frontal areas against invasion. This allocation of resources accurately reflects the imitative pattern of the armed forces of the Republic of Korea [ROK], which include an independent air force and a navy (complete with a marine corps) in a U.S.-style multiservice structure with a JCS [Joint Chiefs of Staff] organization. Obviously the U.S. form of organization that suits a noncontinental power diverts human and material resources from the ground forces, even though Korea—unlike the U.S.—faces a direct land threat at close quarters.

The political condition greatly aggravates the risks that derive from the mismatch between the ROK armed forces as now organized and the specifics of the Korean situation: the North Korean regime is explicitly irredentist as well as totalitarian; indeed, a war of reunification is the governing theme of North Korean policies across the board, whereby the possibilities of economic development are sacrificed to the accumulation of military power. (The ROK allocates under 6 percent for its defense expenditures while the equivalent in the North must be of the order of 20 percent or more; conscription terms compound the difference: 30 months (army) versus five years).

The specific problem that results is that the North is very hard to deter reliably; even the high probability of an ultimate defeat followed by a battered retreat back to the DMZ need not necessarily deter the North. If that regime were to see itself "losing the peace," it might resort to war—if only limited—for the sole purpose of arresting the South's continued economic progress. (The North-South GNP [Gross National Product] ratio is now 1:4; by the beginning of the 1990s it could easily be 1:8.)

Thus a superior defensive capability need not suffice to deter war in the Korean case. In the circumstances, the Republic of Korea requires preclusive security, i.e., much more than the ultimate ability to defeat the North after the fact; the latter would ensure the eventual victory of the South but it could not by itself protect it from the ravages of a war possibly very destructive.

In theory there are three "pure" choices:

First, a preclusive defense: a defense strong enough to defeat invasion (or lesser attacks) right at the start, before serious damage could be inflicted on the Seoul area. Obviously, only ROK forces greatly superior could thus provide deterrence-by-denial, because they would have to outmatch the North Koreans immediately, even in a situation in which the North were to attack by surprise. Very roughly, it may be calculated that to provide a totally preclusive defense the South would need a 3:1 quality/quantity superiority over the North—nothing less would suffice to allow unmobilized and widely distributed forces to defeat immediately a surprise threat concentrated on chosen sectors of the front. Because of its very great cost, such a preclusive defense (which gives automatic deterrence) must be judged as no more than a theoretical alternative at present.

Second, a pre-emptive defense: this would require primarily offensive capabilities, obtained by reducing or eliminating the forces now distributed to provide linear and territorial defenses. Under such a strategy, the South would preclude an invasion by attacking first. Aside from a great increase in offensive capabilities (armored forces, commando forces, very mobile light infantry and attack aviation, as well as long-range rocket artillery, etc.) this strategy would require, in permanence, the political will to strike at gathering North Korean force concentrations before they could be ready to launch their own attacks. This strategy would not of course be acceptable to the United States because, in practice, it would require that the South begin the fighting, thus seemingly starting the war. Moreover, such a strategy is not compatible with the situation that already now exists, because the North is already deployed in a manner that would call for preemption. (Even if such a strategy is rejected out of hand, it should be realized that in the degree that the South is deployed defensively and concentrates its own resources on defensive capabilities, the North remains free to deploy offensively—and that is why its capabilities are now so threatening. If, conversely, the South were deployed offensively, the North would have to begin diluting its offensive strength in order to strengthen its own territorial defenses.)

The final choice is the one that now obtains: Korea relies on American nuclear deterrence to provide preclusive security, even while relying mainly on its own forces to provide the bulk of the defensive strength that would confront a North Korean invasion (or lesser attack) not in fact deterred. U.S nuclear deterrence gains much in credibility from the presence of U.S. troops in Korea and especially those ordinarily deployed north of Seoul. But of course the value of this deterrent depends on the *North Korean* estimate of the likely conduct of the U.S. Government. Obviously, in the event of a North Korean aggression, the choice before the U.S. Government would be very harsh: either confront the enormity of nuclear use to arrest a war as soon as it begins, or else see a war unfold in which an ultimate victory might well be preceded by the substantial destruction of the Seoul area in a sequence of invasion and counteroffensive. It would have been understandable if the North Koreans had estimated that President Carter would not have sanctioned nuclear use in any circumstances, and it is tempting to believe that

U.S. nuclear deterrence is sufficiently credible at present. But of course reliance on nuclear deterrence to provide preclusive security against a non-nuclear threat is not a comfortable condition for either the ROK or the United States.

None of the "pure" alternatives so far examined are satisfactory: a preclusive defense must be judged as excessively costly; a preemptive defense as politically unacceptable; and U.S nuclear deterrance as of uncertain credibility. But there is one more alternative, albeit not "pure," which would provide a sufficient approximation of a truly preclusive level of security: a resilient, fortified, defense-in-depth. Such a defense should not cost too much, it should be politically acceptable to both the United States and Korea, and it would be far more reliable than nuclear deterrence (which would still, however, remain necessary to protect against a North Korean offensive actively supported by the Soviet Union or the PRC). That, obviously, is the type of defense that the ROK ought to have. In fact it is the defense that both the U.S. and ROK authorities may believe they now have. But to actually achieve a genuine defense-in-depth great changes would be needed: budgetary (to reallocate resources to the ground forces); organizational (to drastically restructure the ROK forces as a whole and the ROK army in particular); doctrinal (to reorient the present U.S.-style attrition approach); and in equipment, detailed deployments, and, finally, training.

It would be premature, however, to present a scheme for a resilient defense-in-depth. In view of the prevailing belief that one is already in place, it is first necessary to show why that is not so.

The Problem

The armed forces of the Republic of Korea are well trained and highly motivated. The army is still organized on the model of the U.S. Army of the early 1950s and has triangular regimental structure. Almost all their equipment is of U.S. origin or design, and the training and tactical doctrine of the ROK forces, ground, air, and naval, are directly patterned on U.S. lines (not, however, on the current evolving U.S. model but rather that of the recent past). Thus the ROK forces are largely oriented toward "attrition" warfare, in which primary reliance is placed on firepower to destroy the enemy piecemeal.

The North Korean forces by contrast seem to be primarily maneuver oriented, in both the Soviet style for armor, and the Chinese for the light infantry. Instead of attrition, they would place primary reliance on shock and infiltration in order to set the stage for penetrations and envelopments—to be achieved after the preliminary moves to confuse the enemy command, demoralize his troops, and disrupt the coordination between forces in forward positions and their artillery fire support. The North Korean army includes even more artillery than that of the ROK, but its primary role is to support maneuver tactics by suppression and shock, rather than to reduce the ROK's strength in a static contest of firepower.

This basic difference in the doctrinal orientation of the two armies is reflected in their force structures.* Although the ROK army is smaller (520 thousand vs. 700 thousand), the North Korean has twice the number of maneuver battalions; although these are smaller than comparable ROK battalions, their overall firepower is roughly equal. More generally, the poorer society has the more capital-intensive army: the North Koreans deploy more than twice as many battle tanks (2,200 vs. 860) and also more antitank weapons than the ROK army. In light artillery the two sides are comparable but the North has twice as much larger caliber artillery and three times as many heavy mortars. The North also has some 1,900 multiple rocket launchers, shock-and-suppression weapons *par excellence*. A large part of the ROK Army's strength is deployed close to the DMZ, much of it within artillery range.

ROK defense plans and troop dispositions still largely reflect U.S. threat perceptions. This is not surprising because frequently rotated U.S. Army personnel still dominate the joint command and planning process. These threat perceptions seem to reflect generic U.S. concepts and the NATO conception of the threat and are not particularly responsive to the specifics of the North Korean force structure. A distinctive "Korean" element in the joint U.S.-ROK perception of the threat is the great stress placed on peacetime infiltration. The salient perceived threats are the following:

The Prepared Offensive: In this perception it is envisaged that the North Koreans would attack along the major invasion corridors leading to Seoul, each of which is now defended by a single corps. North Korean regular infantry divisions supported by armor and heavy artillery fires would seek to overwhelm the ROK corps to open the way for a follow-up armored breakthrough to the Seoul area.

---

*Unclassifed data from the 1981–1982 edition of the *Military Balance, 1981–1982*. (London: International Institute for Strategic Studies, 1981), pp. 82–83.

The "Blitzkrieg": This would presume strategic surprise. In the absence of adequate warning, ROK regular forces could not fully man the barrier defenses in the Seoul corridors, and the territorial militia could not carry out its planned task of laying the preplanned minefields. Accordingly, given surprise, it is envisaged that the North Koreans would attempt a classic, high-speed, deep penetration offensive spearheaded by massed formations of battle tanks, to break through the inadequately defended barriers. Because ROK forces are now largely concentrated in forward lines in a defense array that lacks geographic depth, this threat is particularly salient. To be sure, the barriers on the Seoul invasion corridors are laid out in depth, but the defense of the barriers depends in part on troops that are to withdraw line by line to hold them in sequence. Accordingly, it is feared that the high-speed elements of the North Korean "blitzkrieg," as well as infiltrated and air-delivered troops, could seize the barriers before they can be fully manned either by withdrawing frontal troops or reinforcements from the rear. (All of this of course assumes surprise against a nonmobilized defense.)

Hardened Artillery: The large and diversified array of North Korean artillery would of course provide fire support in the context of the above threats. But in addition, it is especially well equipped to neutralize the ROK artillery (on which the defense is very heavily dependent under the current attrition strategy), and it could destroy a significant portion of the forward-deployed ROK forces in a surprise barrage. Much of the North Korean artillery is deployed in (very) hard emplacements that no current U.S. air or ground non-nuclear munitions can reliably destroy. Above all, almost all of the ROK artillery would have to operate within range of North Korean guns to support the front-line defenses. (The Soviet-built 130mm guns in North Korean service outrange all ROK artillery weapons except for the small of 175mm guns.) As a result, the hardened North Korean artillery has a major counterbattery capability, while that of the ROK is very marginal. More serious still, the largely forward-deployed ROK army forces are generally vulnerable to destruction by a concentrated surprise barrage.

Harassment of the Seoul Area: The North Koreans have FROG unguided rockets with a range sufficient to reach Seoul. (In addition it is possible that Soviet-built 180mm gun-howitzers may appear in the North's inventory.) It has been suggested that these weapons might be used for the long-range bombardment of the Seoul area. The harassment of the Seoul area by remote firepower might take place in conjunction with an offensive to demoralize the defense, or, alternatively, it might be employed separately, possibly as a bargaining chip in intrawar negotiations. In any case, high accuracy would not be a requirement for such long-range bombardment (which could not in any case inflict material damage of serious proportions).

The In-depth Infiltration and Guerrilla Threat: In addition to these regular force threat perceptions, it is also believed that the North Koreans might also launch a campaign of sabotage and small-scale guerrilla-type raids against both military and civilian targets in the deep interior of the ROK. Such raids and sabotage missions would in part be carried out by activated in-country sympathizers (rural guerrillas and urban terrorists) but mainly by the troops of the North Korean 8th Special Corps, which consist of different types of commando and light-infantry forces, some specifically trained for air or sea infiltration.

Both the "blitzkrieg" and the in-depth infiltration threat coincide with threats that are salient in the global thinking of the U.S. Army. The threat of rapid offensives by massed armor is now of course identified as the critical threat facing the NATO Central Front (and indeed the response to this threat is the organizing theme of the post-Vietnam changes in the force structure, tactics, and equipment preferences of the U.S. Army). On the other hand, the infiltration and guerrilla threat parallels very exactly the nature of the main tactical problem encountered in Vietnam. There is a tendency in U.S. military thought to "globalize" the salient threats manifest in the chief theaters of action and planning. Thus in examining the specifics of the North Korean threat, it is important to guard against the imposition of imported tactical ideas upon local realities.

The diverse tactical (and operational) threats stressed in U.S.-ROK planning are usually combined in the strategic context of a total-commitment, narrow-front North Korean offensive aimed at the main Seoul invasion corridors.

This perceived strategic threat assumes that a North Korean offensive would be rigidly structured to achieve the maximal political objective, i.e., the seizure of the Seoul area, to be followed by the conquest of the rest of the ROK's territory. It appears that little consideration has been given to the possibility that the North Koreans might opt for a more versatile strategy that would limit initial commitments to achieve a hierarchy of limited political objectives if the maximal objective proves to be unattainable. That possibility is explored below, but for now the prevailing threat perceptions will be accepted on their own terms to assess the tactical and operational responses to the threats as now perceived.

The Current Response to the Threat: A Critique

The Strategic Level

Until a decade ago, joint U.S. ROK war planning was based on a phased withdrawal strategy. This assumed that in the event of full-scale invasion, the ROK would be reinforced from CONUS [continental United States] promptly and on a large scale. The immediate task was accordingly to preserve the integrity of the forces in the ROK, absorbing the momentum of an invasion by trading space for time. (The phased withdrawal strategy was also well suited to the characteristic U.S.-style attrition defense: it was envisaged that the enemy forces would repeatedly have to concentrate in order to attack the successive defense lines, each time becoming vulnerable to massed artillery fire and air attack.)

To the credit of those responsible, the grave defects of this strategy were recognized: First, the central assumption that large-scale troop reinforcements from CONUS would arrive soon was politically very fragile in the post-Vietnam environment; second, the short distances between the DMZ and Seoul meant that a withdrawal would quickly have exposed the capital to artillery bombardment; third, it was realized that the orderly conduct of the withdrawals would place extreme pressure on the morale and cohesion of the U.S. and ROK forces, with the inherent danger of an uncontrollable disintegration through chain-reaction effects on morale.

In any case, a phased withdrawal strategy can only be advantageous if much territory is surrendered in each phase, thus forcing the enemy to carry out a lengthy logistic buildup in the wake of each withdrawal, while forcing the enemy's maneuver echelons to over-extend themselves (thus becoming vulnerable to counterattacks).

Moreover, in the struggle for the political control of the Korean peninsula any territorial losses, however minor, could have had great psychological import, reducing confidence in the ROK government and weakening its bargaining position in the event of intra-war negotiations.

The current defense plans retain phased withdrawal as a fallback option, but emphasize the firm defense of the forward line. At the operational level, the goal is to set the stage for the cumulative attrition of enemy maneuver echelons by artillery fire and air-ground strikes. To implement these plans, ammunition allowances have been doubled for the artillery, and a substantial increase in the number of tubes is underway.

A key aspect of the forward-defense strategy is the much increased emphasis given to the use of fixed, semifixed and expedient antitank obstacles, as well as the deployment of antitank missiles. This was of course a response to the sharp increase in the North Korean armor threat. There is by contrast no signficant reliance on the use of armored forces for counterattack on a front-wide scale. ROK armor is now in part distributed to support the infantry (at the rate of one company per division), and in part allocated to the corps level by single brigades and independent tank battalions, their tasks being to cope with localized penetrations.

There is no doubt that the new strategy has corrected many of the defects that had overtaken the previous strategy. Nevertheless the current strategy appears to be dangerously overspecialized, being severly optimized to respond to a specific strategic threat. The implicit assumption is that the North Koreans would aim, from the start, at maximal political objectives; it does not allow for less direct and more limited North Korean strategies.

First, the current strategy is largely focused on the threat of an all out invasion against the Seoul corridors. A direct offensive whose objective would be to reach Seoul by way of the invasion corridors is indeed the most obvious threat. But precisely to the extent that the strategy is perceived as credible by the North Koreans, the direct offensive aimed at breaching the Seoul corridor defenses becomes the less probable threat. Just as the change in U.S. ROK strategy was a response to changed conditions, both in Korea itself and also in the U.S. politico-strategic environment, so also from the North Korean viewpoint the new defense strategy represented a major change in conditions, which should require in turn a change in North Korean strategy. Such a reorientation might best be achieved by maintaining the option of an offensive along the Seoul invasion corridors, even while actually preparing to attack elsewhere.

Second, the current strategy is critically dependent on the support of massed artillery fires and air-ground strikes to destroy enemy forces by sheer attrition. Even if the main enemy effort does develop in the Seoul sector, the further assumption that the enemy will attack in conveniently targetable massed formations may not be valid. Indeed, to the extent that the firepower of the defense is perceived as formidable, the North Koreans have a corresponding incentive to minimize their vulnerability by adopting avoidance tactics such as night attacks (against positions) and fluid infiltration (to bypass frontal positions).

The North Koreans are now given considerable latitude to use controlled dispersion (firepower avoidance) tactics because the defense is lacking in mobile forces. Although its fixed elements may be strong, the defense is short of agile elements that could use the forward positions and barriers as pivots for mobile counter-infiltration or counterthrust operations. It is often asserted that North Korean troop training and command practices are likely to result in rigid and mechanistic tactics. Nevertheless, the North Koreans could operate in dispersed formations (whose single elements would be inherently weak) or alternatively—to gain a quick decision—they could launch a blitzkrieg without having to accept a large risk, even though both the first form of attack, with its combination of rigidity and exposed flanks, should be very vulnerable to countermaneuver tactics. But artillery and close air support cannot in themselves exploit these potential North Korean vulnerabilities. Only an active defense could—by flanking and circling counterattacks to disrupt major enemy thrusts and annihilate trapped units and by the intercept of smaller infantry penetrations. Present defense tactics would by contrast be essentially passive during the entire initial period of a North Korean offensive, with ROK troops being entirely committed to defend forward positions and barrier systems. Thus even the tactical initiative is conceded from the start to the North Koreans.

The Tactical Level: The Armor Threat and the Antiarmor Response

The North Korean inventory of tanks and armored personnel carriers (APCs) has greatly increased over the last decade. The response to the perceived blitzkrieg threat is evident in the antitank barriers built along the invasion corridors and in the procurement of specialized antitank weapons. Further, the ROK's tank forces are trained and deployed to operate primarily in an antitank blocking (and attrition) mode. Partly no doubt because of political reasons, but also as a reflection of U.S. military thought, of the 1950s, the ROK's armor has not been configured to operate in an offensive countermaneuver role, where its task would be to oppose North Korean armor by flanking attacks, temporarily advancing beyond the DMZ if necessary. (Only during the final "eject and pursue" phase of a successful defense would ROK armor operate offensively—and even then only in support of the infantry.)

The allocation of major resources to build antitank barriers on the Seoul invasion corridors was obviously a prudent investment. Much more questionable is the assumption that North Koreans would rely on massed armor to spearhead an invasion—and the resulting emphasis given to this particular threat in formulating ROK equipment choices.

It should be noted that the North Korean inventory of battle tanks is not concentrated in all-armor "mailed fist" formations on the Soviet model. Nor is the terrain suitable for effective armor tactics, whose essence is to use cross-country mobility to avoid the enemy's main strength rather than to make frontal attacks. In Korean conditions, massed formations of armor would be canalized by the terrain into predictable avenues of advance; in the presence of an enemy equipped with antitank weapons, effective armor operations must by contrast exploit their mobility to attack from unexpected directions. That the Korean tank inventory is divided into three roughly equal parts, only one of which consists of massed armor, strongly suggests that the blitzkrieg capability may be no more than a secondary adjunct to infantry operations.

The definition of the prospective North Korean use of armor is of direct relevance to ROK force planning and equipment choices. The priority accorded to the mass armor threat should reflect the more limited operational potential indicated by the North Korean force structure, rather than a conceptualized blitzkrieg threat whose dimensions are set by the total number of battle tanks in the North Korean inventory. In practice, this means that scarce foreign exchange should not be overallocated to meet the armored threat. It is clearly essential to maintain the current barriers, and indeed they ought to be manned continuously as a hedge against a surprise attack. But the procurement of rather expensive and narrowly specialized antitank weapons such as TOW and DRAGON should be limited; instead more versatile light-gun systems, which are effective against infantry as well as armor, should be bought to complement the antitank missiles.

In spite of the prominence of the armor threat, the ROK ground forces are still lacking in modern armor-defeating weapons. No doubt because of the wholesale adoption of the U.S. (infantry) organization as a model, armor-defeating weapons not favored by the U.S. Army are absent from the ROK's inventory. Thus the latter does not contain gun-armed tank destroyers, low-pressure antitank guns, or, for that matter, conventional (full-recoil) antitank guns. Instead there has been an exclusive reliance on rocket launchers and recoilless rifles, in spite of their clear inferiority to low-pressure guns. Similarly, the procurement of antitank missiles had to await their very belated production by the United States, in spite of the fact that

British, French, and German antitank missiles were available long before.

At the Tactical Level: The Hardened Artillery Threat and the Counter-Battery Problem

The most striking inconsistency in the current defense posture is its especially great reliance on artillery against an enemy whose own artillery has a greatly superior counter-battery capability. It is not just the numerical superiority of North Korean artillery that is of decisive importance, but rather its combination of hardened emplacements with superior ranges. Thus even if the present threat perceptions and the current tactical orientation are both accepted in their own terms, the inadequacy of the ROK artillery means that current defense plans could not be implemented effectively. An increase in the number of artillery weapons, which merely expands the inventory, would not solve the problem.

Though rather old, Soviet-pattern guns and gun-howitzers in the 122mm, 152mm, and 130mm calibers outrange the U.S.-built 105mm, 155mm, and 8-inch howitzers of the ROK. (The only modern long-range guns in ROK service are a few 175mm self-propelled M-107s; these outrange even the Soviet 130mm guns, but it is well known that the M-107 is technically unsatisfactory.)

U.S. and ROK air power cannot overcome the counter-battery problem. Much North Korean artillery is deployed in firing positions excavated as through-tunnels in the hills facing the DMZ. Guided air-to-ground weapons of the Maverick type could in theory be used against these targets, but the prior need to suppress air defenses, the sheer number of targets, and target designation problems in the face of obfuscation by smoke, camouflage, and deception would all prevent the execution of an artillery-suppression campaign sufficiently quickly to enable the defense to use its own artillery to full effect.

Aside from the counter-battery problem, it should also be noted that the present ROK artillery inventory is not efficient in terms of the current operational requirements. The replacement of the large number of 105mm howitzers now in ROK service with multiple rocket-launchers and modern 120mm/160mm mortars would result in a great increase in effectiveness.

At the Tactical Level: The In-depth Infiltration and Guerrilla Threat

The North Koreans deploy large numbers of light troops that are specially trained for infiltration and commando-style operations.

The 8th Special Corps is organized to carry out such operations in the deep rear of the ROK, possibly in conjunction with sabotage actions by in-country guerrilla and terrorist elements. But the 8th Special Corps accounts for less than half of the total number of commando-style light troops deployed by the North Koreans. Each front-line division has an organic "light infantry" battalion and each front-line corps has two light infantry brigades. These forces, also trained for infiltration, are not assigned to the 8th Special Corps.

The force structure suggests that although the light troops of the 8th Special Corps would be infiltrated into the ROK by air or by sea for sabotage and raids in the deep interior, the other light troops would mostly infiltrate on foot, in direct support of conventional operations mounted by regular forces.

The ROK response to the in-depth infiltration and guerrilla threat as current perceived is evident in the deployment of active-army counter infiltration battalions and in the wartime provision of Homeland Reserve Divisions. These forces are to be distributed along the coastal areas of the ROK and in its deep interior. But there appears to be no specific response to the shallow infiltration threat in the frontal area, even though standard rear-area security measures are hardly likely to suffice for this purpose. Such measures are not designed to cope with the infiltration of large numbers of enemy troops.

An Alternative Definition of the Threat

There is no disagreement over the capabilities present in the North Korean force structure, but these can be operationalized in terms of a strategy and tactics that differ considerably from those envisaged in current U.S.-ROK perceptions of the threat. The alternative strategy and tactics presented below are: consistent with local military traditions (unlike the established threat perceptions, which largely reflect the Soviet model); responsive to the political context in which North Korea must operate (unlike the established threat perceptions, which appear to ignore political factors); and fully congruent with the specific capabilities found in the North Korean force structure (unlike the established threat perceptions, which discount the role of the exceptionally large light infantry element).

It cannot be claimed that this alternative perception corresponds to North Korean war plans, but in any case, the alternative here defined is a suitable and necessary test of the versatility and robustness of the defense.

The tactical concepts here imputed to the North Koreans are extensions of Chinese tactics developed in the 1930s to overcome the material superiority of the Japanese, and of Japanese tactics designed to obtain high combat results from highly-stretched forces. In essence, these tactics embody a fluid-maneuver approach to infantry warfare and are specifically designed to evade the power of enemy artillery as well as the strength of prepared positions. Against defenses whose flanks are loose, this maneuver approach (usually in the form of circle and block tactics) has historically proved very effective as in the Japanese invasion of Malaya in 1941-1942, in the 1950 North Korean and Chinese offensives in Korea itself, and in the Sino-Indian Himalayan fighting of 1962.

Fluid-maneuver tactics are particularly suited to the Korean terrain. The sharp mountain contours, with their scrubby vegetation, countless gullies, and much broken terrain, do not present serious obstacles to the infiltration of light infantry forces if these are suitably conditioned and trained. At the same time, the terrain has a sponge-like effect on the manpower of the defense: very short fields of fire and observation impose high manpower demands, requiring a very large number of troops to implement a strong linear defense.

Owing to a hypersensitive response to the peacetime infiltration threat, the ROK has been induced to place the bulk of its front-line forces virtually on the DMZ line itself, so that the nominal Combat Outpost Line is in fact virtually identical to the forward edge of the battle area. The ROK army tries to reproduce the structure of the old-style U.S. Army linear defense with its two-up-and-one-back formula, but the terrain and the wide frontages have forced many ROK divisions to depart from this. In one (extreme case, a single battalion is holding 16 kms of frontage. Similarly, the ROK's artillery is also deployed well forward, much of it being within a few kilometers of the DMZ.

The relatively small number of actual maneuver units in the force structure (a common malady of forces patterned on the U.S. model), the absorptive terrain, the strategic imperative of a forward defense, the political demand for total security from infiltration, all combine to result in a thin cordon defense. This is inherently vulnerable to fluid maneuver penetrations because mountain flanks are not solidly held and reserves are few. (Most reserves are tied down in blocking positions astride vehicular approaches or in terrain-dominating hilltop positions.)

If North Korean infiltration and fluid-maneuver tactics are employed against the thinly manned First Republic of Korea Army (FROKA) sector on the eastern half of the peninsula, parts of those frontal defenses could collapse, quite easily opening axes of advance against the flanks of the main ROK forces deployed in the Seoul invasion corridors. If the main forces of the defense then come under attack from the front as well, they could then be overrun. If, on the other hand, the FROKA defenses do not collapse, multiple penetrations by light infantry units could still occur, and these may induce the ROK government to divert significant forces from the invasion corridors to the FROKA sector—thus facilitating a subsequent North Korean offensive against Seoul.

Well-trained light infantry suitably employed will be relatively impervious to artillery and air attack, and because the ROK army does not have a sufficient number of agile light units, the defense is in general ill-prepared to cope with the frontal infiltration threat.

Accordingly, North Korean light troops which are not part of the 8th Special Corps could be employed effectively for the preliminary infiltration and disruption of the battlefield. The initial infiltration moves might be timed to precede the overt outbreak of hostilities by the regular forces (e.g., infiltration could begin at dusk, for a dawn H-hour). During that interval, North Korean light troops could penetrate to depths of up to 10kms. or so, simply bypassing ROK frontal defense positions to uncouple the indirect fire support on which the defense of ROK forward positions so heavily depends. They could do this by cutting telephone wires and by firing upon or by launching close-quarter attacks against the artillery batteries that are supposed to support the ROK frontal positions. (This would be supplemented by the jamming of front-line radio communications after H-hour.) Infiltrated light infantry could also ambush reinforcements and supply vehicles as well as any retreating forces. They could also take up firing positions in the rear of ROK frontline defenses to simulate encirclement.

Upon the overt outbreak of hostilities, ROK frontal positions would come under very heavy artillery fire, and would also be threatened (if not actually attacked) by regular forces approaching toward them. At this point, when the ROK defense would call upon its artillery for fire support, the combined effects of jamming, wire-cutting, and of direct or fire assaults against howitzer and mortar batteries would become manifest. Unexpectedly deprived of the fire support on which the defense now so greatly relies, ROK troops manning forward positions could also come under the fire (from unexpected directions) of infiltrated fire teams. That is unlikely to be significantly destructive, but it could be very demoralizing.

The immediate tactical goal of the North Koreans would be to undermine the confidence of the front-line forces. This could precipitate imprudent withdrawals (which would then be ambushed) or, at least, it would induce ROK command echelons to send up reinforcements hurriedly (and these would be ambushed also).

In such an indirect, multiphase strategy, North Korean regular infantry and armored forces would only launch determined attacks against positions that actually block desired axes of penetration. Elsewhere, North Korean regular forces would merely maintain the appearance of a threat against the vehicular approaches with feints and demonstrations during the first phase.

Instead, regular infantry forces would seek to penetrate cross country, bypassing the heavily defended barrier systems along the vehicular approaches by way of the higher ground. North Korean attacks upon ROK frontal positions that cannot be bypassed conveniently would mostly take place at night, with silent approaches and the use of "hugging" tactics to negate air and artillery support.

Such infantry-only penetrations would seek to reach and disrupt the divisional rear areas, but most of the forces involved would peel off to outflank and attack the ROK forces deployed to guard the vehicular approaches against frontal attacks. North Korean armor would not actually attack the vehicular-approach defenses until the combination of preliminary infiltration by light infantry and the stronger regular infantry penetrations would have undermined the integrity of the defenses as a whole. North Korean armor would then be sent in to accelerate and deepen the penetrations. However, tanks and vehicles in general would play only a secondary role in these tactics until the final stage of *coup de grace,* because, unlike the light infantry or the regular infantry operating in a fluid maneuver mode, vehicles would unavoidably be vulnerable to artillery fire and air attack.

The most important feature of the alternative North Korean strategy here envisaged is its political flexibility: the offensive would be structured as a multiphase operation, with each phase entailing a strictly limited commitment of strength and a limited degree of strategic exposure in proportion to the political gains that each phase might separately be expected to achieve.

During its first—infiltration—phase, the fighting would have the general character of a large-scale border incident, at least from the viewpoint of observers remote from the scene, including policy-makers in Washington, Moscow and Peking.

If the U.S. reaction to this first phase of the offensive is unexpectedly strong, or if ROK defenses prove to be much more resilient than expected, or if the PRC or Moscow apply strong pressures upon them to cease and desist, the North Koreans may then abandon wider offensive intentions. Instead they would try to secure limited political and diplomatic gains by calling for a cease-fire in place. At this pont, their main forces would still be intact but they might have made some (minor) territorial gains in some sectors. (And even very modest territorial conquests could generate significant benefits for the North, by undermining South Korean confidence in the ROK regime, and by inducing a collapse in investor confidence.) A North Korean offer of a prompt cease-fire would place the onus of continuing the fighting upon the United States and the ROK. Domestic U.S. and world opinion might well react unfavorably to the pursuit of a dangerous conflict for the sake of territory that might seem insignificant to non-Koreans.

If, on the other hand, both the external political circumstances and the military situation develop more favorably, the North Koreans would then launch the second phase of the offensive by sending in the regular infantry, albeit not at first against the major vehicular approaches. If a chain-reaction effect on moral does not materialize and the defenses do not collapse, local territorial gains by the North Koreans might still induce the ROK to redeploy forces from the Seoul invasion corridors to carry out reconquest operations. The military risks of doing so would be obvious, but the very possibility of a limited scope North Korean offensive would confront the ROK leadership with a very difficult choice between the political necessity of avoiding territorial losses and military prudence.

If the North Koreans then choose to go on, even localized penetrations would open the way for further flanking moves against the essential barrier defenses of the Seoul invasion corridors.

In the third phase the main forces would come under heavy North Korean artillery fire, while the ROK's artillery would be reduced by a major counter-battery effort (notably employing the very accurate 130mm guns housed in hard emplacements). Next, North Korean regular infantry still employing fluid-maneuver tactics would be sent into action. The aim of those forces would be to seize or at least disrupt the barrier-systems laid out in depth between Seoul and the DMZ.

The main defenses guarding the Seoul area would thus come under heavy fire and would be attacked on the ground simultaneously from the front and from the flanks. (North Korean 8th Special Corps troops might also try to attack the barriers by vertical envelopment.) The psychological effect of these North Korean attacks upon the Seoul frontal defenses would be compounded by the harrassment of the entire sector (all the way back to Seoul) by FROG rockets and long-range artillery (possibly using RAP rounds) to further intensify the effects on morale.

Even then, in the third phase, the North Koreans might suspend their offensive—if the U.S. PRC, (or Soviet) reaction is too strong to be resisted, or if the ROK defense is too strong. At this point the North Koreans could revert to a cease-fire-in-place option, with the additional bargaining chips of any more localized gains as well as their now proven capability to bombard the Seoul area at long range. Obviously, these military gains could be exploited politically and diplomatically in the context of intrawar negotiations. The bulk of high value North Korean forces, that is the tank and motorized divisions, would still be intact and uncommitted.

Alternatively, the North Koreans might pursue maximal political objectives in a final fourth phase, by launching their tank-heavy main forces against the Seoul defenses, whose barrier systems laid out in depth would by then have been weakened by multiple forms of attack. Thus the envisaged blitzkrieg threat would then finally materialize after all, but only as the *coup de grace*.

In Conclusion

It will have been noted that throughout the discussion no mention has been made of the air and naval forces. Much of the problem of Korea's defense— and much of the solution too—could be found in this omission.

Now it is true that there are North Korean air threats (for example, an initial, surprise bombardment) and naval threats too (submarine attacks, and mining—also by submarines). In addition, there is likely to be air-delivered and seaborne infiltration. But all such threats are either insignificant (see the payloads of North Korean aircraft) or not of urgent effect (a mine blockade), or else neither as significant nor as urgent when compared to the brutally direct threat of an invasion of the northern parts of the ROK—especially of the Seoul area where more than 8 million people and their great industrial achievements are now at risk.

The feeble and secondary air and naval threats should warrant at most an air-defense response on the one hand and a coastal-defense response on the other. These are functions that could well be fulfilled by a small and cheap air corps headed perhaps by a one-star general, and even cheaper sea corps of similar stature without need for the elaborate command structures, headquarters, and ancillary services now in place. The latter could only be justified if the air and naval forces of the ROK could contribute urgently and significantly to the territorial defense of the ROK, but this they cannot do.

In theory, air support could contribute to the ground defense, but to do that the North Korean antiaircraft forces must first be suppressed—whereas the help of airpower would be needed most at the very beginning of war (especially if the North Koreans in fact surprise an unmobilized ROK). But more fundamentally, only a very large air force with the most sophisticated weapons (though with rather simple aircraft) could be truly useful in the Korean context because the salient forms of the threat—light infantry infiltration, regular infantry in a fluid mode, and the heavily fortified artillery—are largely immune to conventional forms of fighter-bomber attack. Certainly the Mach 2 fighters that the ROK Air Force passionately desires could contribute very little to the territorial defense of the nation. (To use $20 million F-16s to attack North Korean armor heavily defended by antiaircraft guns would be very wasteful in aircraft and would probably yield insignificant results.) Nor could the destroyer and corvett navy of the ROK play a significant role in the defense of the territory.

A day will come when the ROK will have achieved an adequate level of security against invasion. Then it should indeed acquire a first-class air force and a blue-water navy—if only to contribute to the coalition defense of the North-East Pacific region. But at present, the diversion of scarce funds into imitative air and naval forces of scant immediate defensive values is a very grave mistake: no man should purchase caviar when he cannot provide enough rice to feed his family.

Another diversion of resources that is premature is the heavy ROK investment in military industries. Now it is obviously advantageous for the ROK to manufacture anything that it can in fact manufacture economically—and the list of arms that are cheaper made than bought obviously becomes longer as the Korean economy develops. But it is inexcusable to allocate large funds to produce "Korean" major weapons when these same funds could be used much more productively to modernize weapons in hand or import modern weapons from elsewhere. (The ROK could fully modernize three M-47 tanks for the price of each new Korean-made tank.) Again, in a secure future, the ROK might benefit from its own high-technology military industries, but that time is not yet.

The larger issue that comprises all these points is the complex interaction between the United States and the ROK in the realm of security. The alliance brings great benefits to both countries. (It is indeed a very equitable arrangement because the United States would derive enormous benefit from its Korean presence in a variety of global conflict scenarios.) For the ROK the alliance provides a very necessary element of deterrence, even though the ROK provides most of its own defense. But on the other hand, the alliance also generates a false sense of security, while the uncritical acceptance of U.S. models of organization and tactics has greatly distorted Korean military priorities. Only an original Korean strategy, an original force structure, and terrain-suited and resource-suited operational methods could assure an adequate level of security at a tolerable cost. A Korean-style defense-in-depth strategy would require much effort and expenditure, but in the context of an overall restructuring of the armed forces, it could turn out to be much more economical overall—and it would certainly be much more robust than the present combination of a cordon defense and U.S. nuclear deterrence.

2

JAPANESE SECURITY RESPONSIBILITY: KOREAN PERSPECTIVES

Bae-Ho Hahn, *Korea University*

Since the end of World War II, Japan has successfully achieved a set of foreign policy goals envisioned by the late Prime Minister Yoshida Shigeru. In conducting its foreign policy, Japan has adhered to Yoshida's guiding principles, which consisted of a major emphasis on the nation's economic reconstruction by means of expanded trade with all countries; an economically viable Japan, which, with U.S. help, must play an important role in developing a non-Communist Asia; and an independent Japan as a member of the United Nations, thereby enhancing Japan's status in international society.

In implementing its foreign policy, these broad guiding principles have been supplemented by more specific working rules that called for Japan to expand the overseas market by means of economic diplomacy, to avoid more than minimum defense spending, to avoid involvement in international political disputes, to avoid resorting to the use of force when involved in disputes, and to reduce actual or potential international tensions through diplomatic means.

During the immediate postwar period and throughout the heyday of the Cold War era, both the principles and the working rules represented the prevailing pacifist mood in Japan and the constitutional restraints that renounced "war as a sovereign right of the nation and the threat or use of force as a means of settling international disputes, and the possession of land, sea, and air forces, as well as other war potential." As a result, Japan's economy has achieved unparalleled growth, it has been able to develop constructive economic and political relations with its neighbors, and its democratic institutions have flourished. Moreover, in achieving this remarkable economic growth, Japan has enjoyed not only easy access to imported raw materials and food at reasonable prices, but also a relatively stable international political environment in which it could conduct its affairs.

The events of the mid-1970s highlighted by the Vietnam reversal and the oil crisis, however, have transformed this environment based on the strategic superiority of the United States' over the Soviet Union. With the establishment of diplomatic relations between the United States and the People's Republic of China and the entry of the PRC as a major factor in the international scene, the interaction among the major powers has become much more complex than in the 1950s and 1960s. The oil crisis presented Japan with yet another challenge that could not be easily met in the context of Japan's past foreign policy orientation.

For Japan, the 1970s was therefore a decade of uncertainty. Confronted with mounting criticism from its Western allies and developing countries over its economic behavior and trade policy and faced with rising oil prices and a radical shift in the balance of power policy in the region, Tokyo began to have serious doubts about its postwar policy of economic growth and passive diplomacy.

Characteristically, Japan has passively accepted the challenge to change its existing policies on defense spending and trade, but pays only lipservice to the need to take initiatives to meet these challenges. The reasons for this may be variously ascribed to the postwar structure of Japanese politics, the national psychology, the traumatic experience of the past, the special relationship with the United States, and also to the benefits gained from a passive diplomatic posture of the past. But whatever the reason, it is clear that Japan can no longer base its foreign and economic policies on the circumstances of the past. "The 1980s," said Hahn, "will force Japan to make crucial choices in some major issue areas."

The Need for Consensus

In the postwar period *kiene-tsukuri*, or nation-making, served the purpose of coalescing diverse and heterogeneous social and political views into accepting tasks required for Japan's national reconstruction and of legitimizing the conservative rule within the framework of the newly adopted constitution. In achieving this consensus, the conservative government was assisted by an unprecedented rate of economic growth and by the improved status of the country in the international community. In the area of national defense, however, the conservatives have not been able to obtain a broad national consensus.

In part, this failure to reach a broad national consensus can be attributed to the attempt by some ultra conservatives to turn back time by proposing a "national reconstruction plan," which, if carried out, would have nullified some of the major reforms instituted during the occupation period. The plan included amending the constitution to remove the restrictive "peace" clause, reorganizing the police forces in favor of control by the central government, and revising the electoral system in favor of a single member district system. Suspecting the conservatives of having ulterior motives in proposing this plan, the leftist parties completely rejected the recommendations, with the result that the political forces in Japan became hopelessly divided into two opposing camps.

In recent years, however, a substantial change has taken place in the attitudes and opinions of the Japanese public as well as in the stance of political parties on the question of defense and national security. The most notable change has been in the position of the centrist opposition parties, such as Komeito and the Democratic Socialist Party, which renounced their opposition to the U.S.-Japan Security Treaty and endorsed the conservative Liberal Democratic Party's (LDP's) security policy by agreeing to support the maintenance of the Self Defense Forces (SDF) and the Mutual Security Treaty with the United States "for the time being." Even the Japanese Socialist Party appears to be moving toward acceptance of the need for the SDF. To some extent, this has taken the edge off the sharp confrontation between the conservatives and the leftists. Nevertheless, given the past performance of the LDP, the nature of Japan's decision-making process, and the general state of Japanese politics, it is unlikely that any radical change in Japan's defense policy will occur, or that a broad national consensus on the nature of its responsibilities will be reached in the foreseeable future.

In spite of the reluctance of Japanese policymakers to initiate a radical change in Japan's defense posture, it seems inevitable, Hahn stated, that substantial modifications will need to be made in the working rules applied in the implementation of its foreign policy in the 1980s. This is now necessary, he said, not as a result of pressures for change from within, but because external events are forcing the Japanese to reexamine the foundations of their diplomatic and security policies.

Until recent years, the Japanese could afford to be concerned exclusively with safeguarding their independence and prosperity.

Feeling little responsibilty for maintaining, let alone defending, a world order that allowed Japan to prosper while others were embroiled in conflict, Japan saw no reason to change the premises of its foreign, economic, and security policies. But the situation has changed. With the near outbreak of a Korean war in 1975, the eventual withdrawal of U.S. troops from Asia as implied in the Nixon Doctrine, the accelerated Soviet military buildup in the eastern part of Siberia and on the northern islands close to Gokkaido, and the oil crisis in 1973, the Japanese became sharply aware of their vulnerability. This was expressed in the fear of many that Japan would not be able to sustain its economic prosperity and that the continued Soviet buildup in the region might dangerously expose Japan to Soviet pressures and blackmail, perhaps to the point of neutrality. No doubt in response to this threat a constitutional revision draft has reportedly been completed by an LDP committee calling for the abolition of a part of the peace clause and the insertion of a provision that the "Self Defense Forces shall be maintained for safeguarding the peace and independence of Japan and for the security of our country." Furthermore, the draft reportedly calls for the prime minister, on behalf of the Cabinet, to exercise his supreme control over the SDF, to declare a state of emergency with the approval of the Diet when necessary, and to mobilize the SDF in that event.

In all likelihood, Hahn predicted, the proposed LDP revision "will revive heated security debates in Japan, and will move the focus of the debate decisively from discussions about the constitutional and legal inhibitions to the issue of institutionalization of control over the SDF and possibly about conversion of the SDF into normal armed forces." Such a debate, he said, will not only make such discussions far more relevant to the changing realities in Japan's external environment, but it may also perhaps create a climate so that Japanese leaders can persuade the Japanese public to accept a larger military role.

Japan's Expanded Role in U.S.-Japanese Security Relations

The debate on the issue of Japan's national security has been reflected in the composition of the Self Defense Forces. Firmly adhering to the peace clause in the constitution that renounced "war as a sovereign right of the nation and the threat or use of force as a means of settling international disputes," Japan's military has been limited in its role to providing a small, local defense capability to cope with small-scale contingencies. For a while such a capability met Japan's defense requirements. However, in time, some began to question the effectiveness of such a limited defense force. Sakata Mitchida, former director general of the Defense Agency, was one such person. Acknowledging the limitations imposed on the SDF by the constitution and by public sentiment, he proposed the concept of a "Basic Standing Force." Essentially, the concept called for a "small but flexible force which was capable of not only being able to deal with a small scale contingency as a total defense system, but also of being able to expand as the need arose. In fact what Sakata Mitchida called for was a qualitative improvement rather than a quantitative expansion of the SDF.

When the concept of a Basic Standing Force was formulated, it was based on the following assumptions about the strategic environment around Japan:
1. The United States and the Soviet Union will try to avoid an intercontinental nuclear war and an armed conflict that might lead to their full-scale involvement.
2. The Soviet Union will still have to take into account the possibility of a NATO-Warsaw Pact confrontation.
3. A gradual improvement in Sino-Soviet relations will not lead to an end of confrontation.
4. The status quo will be maintained on the Korean peninsula.
5. Improvements in Sino-American relations will continue on a reciprocal basis.

The possibility of a Soviet invasion could not be ruled out completely; nevertheless, Japanese defense planners considered it highly unlikely that such an invasion would take place, if only because the cost of mounting the attack would outweigh the advantages of occupying the country. Besides, this would presuppose an armed conflict between the United States and the Soviet Union in which a conventional occupation of Japan would be the last thing either would attempt.

The continuing buildup of Soviet military forces around Japan, Hahn pointed out, increasingly calls into question the tenability of these assumptions. At the same time, it raises serious doubts about Japan's ability to counter the Soviet threat. According to many defense analysts, the SDF is at a distinct disadvantage. With 75 percent of the equipment in the Ground Self Defense Force of 1960s vintage or earlier, they predict it will take Japan at least 10 years at the current rate to modernize its forces to at least the 1970-era level of equipment. For similar reasons, the Japanese air and sea defense capabilities are also considered highly inadequate to cope with the

Soviet threat—as illustrated by Japan's failure to identify and intercept the MiG-25 piloted by a Soviet defector in 1976. Not surprisingly, then, Japan's defense analysts point out that the most urgent need for Japan is to replace the existing air defense network and to acquire a greater tactical air power.

It is unlikely that there will be any radical change in either the composition or role of the SDF, however, as successive attempts by U.S. administrations to persuade Japan to increase its defense spending and to accept a bigger role in the security of the region have shown. To many Americans, the Japanese position is both frustrating and difficult to understand. For their part, the Japanese see little reason to spend more than 1 percent of their GNP on national defense. Currently allocating more than $10 billion annually on defense, up 16 percent over 1970, Japan's defense budget is already the seventh and eighth largest in the world. The Soviet naval buildup and threat to the safety of the seal lanes extending from the Middle East is the responsibility of the United States, Japanese declare.

As Hahn pointed out, only Japan itself can decide on the value of playing a bigger role in the security of the region and that, Hahn stated, depends on whether or not the security environment around Japan permits it to remain ambivalent about the Soviet threat.

Japan's Role in the Security of Korea

U.S. inability to understand Japan's reluctance to assume an active security role in Northeast Asia is shared by the South Koreans. The maintenance of peace and stability on the Korean peninsula benefits South Korea, they concede, but does it not also benefit Japan? "In their minds," said Hahn, "the Japanese have been only reaping the fruits of peace at the expense of the toil and sacrifices of the Korean people." Clearly, the South Koreans believe Japan should do more.

From the Japanese perspective, Japan is already playing a vital role in the security of South Korea. By being politically stable and economically powerful, a former director general of the Japanese Defense Agency contended, Japan is relatively secure from external threat. And if Japan is secure, he said, then Korea is secure. Responding to this, Hahn declared that Japan had clearly turned around the argument about Japan's being a beneficiary of the U.S.-ROK security arrangement and by asserting that Korea benefits from the U.S.-Japan security relationship. The fact, Hahn said, is that all three parties involved are beneficiaries of these security arrangements and all three are obligated to assume responsibilities for their own security as well as for the security at the regional level. Furthermore, he declared, they are also obligated to develop a close collaborative effort to enhance that peace and stability to this end. Japan must take an active part in the security of South Korea.

Conclusions

In the last few years, the Japanese have become increasingly aware of the Soviet Union's expanding military strength in the Far East and of the importance of defense cooperation between the United States and Japan. As support for the Self Defense Forces has increased, the focus of the security debate seems to have shifted from the question of whether or not military policies were violating the constitution to the question of the permissible range of military activities and of what military capabilities are desirable, given the constitutional constraints, in the face of the increased Soviet threat. Outlining the course Japan must now take, Hahn said: "The challenge of Japan's leaders is one of guiding the Japanese public into accepting security responsibilities, not necessarily by moving sharply away from the principles but by significantly modifying the working rules which have guided past Japanese foreign policy, not by departing from the course Japan has successfully followed for these years, but to build on it a broad-based national consensus relevent to the realities of the international environment."

As a first step, Hahn called for the development of harmony and cordial relations between Japan and South Korea. If this is achieved, he said, the United States will be able to perform its tasks with greater effectiveness, and peace and stability in Northeast Asia will be greatly enhanced.

3

JAPANESE SECURITY RESPONSIBILITY

Michael Blaker, *Director, Japanese Studies, CSIS*

The common belief that Japan is an economic giant but a military pygmy is scarcely true, Dr. Michael Blaker asserted. Since the Self Defense Forces (SDF) were organized in 1954, Japan has rearmed substantially. In the last 25 years, its annual defense-related expenditures have risen 15-fold, to about $10 billion. This has placed Japan ninth in the world in the amount of money spent on national defense, ahead of North Korea, South Korea, the Philippines, and Taiwan. More than 240 thousand Japanese serve in the increasingly well-equipped air, maritime, and land services. Japanese airforce pilots fly, or soon will fly, F-15 fighters, P3C antisubmarine aircraft, and Grumman E2C Hawkeye radar reconnaissance planes. At the present time, there are fewer Japanese warships than a decade ago, but they are bigger, more heavily armed, and total naval tonnage is higher. Land forces have more firepower and mobility. Japan's land forces also include helicopters, armed personnel carriers, and tanks, many of which are Japanese made.

Criticism of Japan's Self-Defense

Despite these positive trends in defense planning, Japan is nevertheless spending a smaller percentage of its national budget and GNP on defense than it was before. In 1954, military outlays took up 14 percent of the national budget; in 1978, they made up only 5.4 percent. As a percentage of GNP, military outlays have fallen from 1.78 percent in 1954 to 0.9 percent in 1978. By these standards, Japan's defense spending is lower than that of any other major nation.

Other criticisms leveled at the Self Defense Force pertain to its manpower and purpose. Staff salaries, critics point out, account for nearly 60 percent of the total defense budget, of which only 20 percent is allocated for arms and equipment. Furthermore, critics say, the quality of military training and the level of preparedness of the SDF is low. To support their position, they cite the failure of Japanese radar in 1977 to detect the entry into Hokkaido of a Soviet MiG-25 fighter piloted by a young lieutenant seeking asylum in the West. Such weaknesses once led former U.S. Ambassador to Japan Edwin O. Reischauer to dismiss the SDF as a "psychological security blanket."

In a sense that is true; although Japan's military forces are designed to safeguard its territory against a small-scale conventional attack and to maintain domestic security, they in fact only supplement those forces of the United States—even for the defense of Japanese territory. In this respect, Japan, under the provisions of the Treaty of Cooperation and Mutual Security with the United States, is obliged to provide bases and other facilities in Japan for the United States to use to protect "the security of the Far East"; to consult with the United States if the peace and security of the Far East is jeopardized; and to contribute substantially to the costs of maintaining the United States military presence on Japanese soil.

Frustrated by Japan's reluctance to assume a greater role, critics argue that the amount Japan allocates to defense depends on three factors—the seriousness of the threat facing Japan; the degree of faith Japanese have in the U.S. commitment to defend Japan; and the level of domestic support in Japan for defense activity.

Facts, however, refute this case, Dr. Blaker argued. Over time, increases in Japanese defense spending have taken place slowly and steadily, without a direct connection to events either inside or outside Japan. For instance, despite the detonation of an atomic bomb by the PRC in 1958 and the Sino-Soviet split in the late 1960s and despite the deployment of huge Chinese and Soviet military forces facing each other along their common border, the outbreak of the Vietnam War, and the recent Soviet military buildup in Asia, Japan has not sharply increased its defense spending.

This holds true even at a time when the Japanese have begun seriously to question the U.S. commitment to the region. According to recent opinion polls, more than half the Japanese do not think the United States would act to protect Japan—a figure 10 percent higher than a decade ago. The Nixon "shocks" of 1971, the U.S. withdrawal from Vietnam, and the proposed removal of U.S. ground troops from South Korea have raised doubts about the firmness of U.S. commitment in the minds of Japanese, Blaker believes.

Most significant of all, perhaps, is that, although the Japanese public and the opposition parties are now far more supportive of their government's defense policy than in the past (in fact, 86 percent of those polled in 1978 supported a Japanese defensive military capability), Japan still has refrained from engaging in a massive military buildup, as some—at least on this side of the Pacific—would hope.

Factors Preventing a Rapid Buildup

There are several reasons why Japan has not greatly increased its defense spending, in spite of U.S. prodding to do so, according to Dr. Blaker. First, there is a Japanese sense of isolation and vulnerability. The expansion of Japan's forces might be regarded by its enemies as a hostile act and thus encourage a preemptive strike against Japan. Second, there remains the legacy of Hiroshima and Nagasaki and all the other traumatic memories of Japan's defeat in World War II. Third, there is a belief that Japan has prospered without large-scale military forces that might alienate foreign markets or suppliers of vital raw materials. Fourth, a large military budget draws funds away from the other sectors of the economy. And last, there is the fear that the United States might alter its policies after Japan becomes commited to a more active defense policy.

Clearly, the composition of the Self Defense Forces is in accord with public sentiments. Except for a few ultra-rightists, as Dr. Blaker commented, "virtually no one in Japan presses for Japan to build nuclear weapons, few push for significantly higher defense spending or large-scale rearmament, and you can count on no one urging the undertaking of any military commitments that might embroil Japan in some foreign conflict."

Notwithstanding this general consensus, several issues in Japanese defense policy remain, preventing total agreement. They are the status of U.S. military bases and personnel in Japan, the relationship of U.S. nuclear weapons to Japanese security, and the scope of Japan's obligations under the Mutual Security Treaty to assist the United States in maintaining peace and security in the Far East. These issues cannot be ignored, Blaker warned, because "it has been disagreement on these questions that has provoked whatever serious domestic debate has taken place on defense-related matters.

And it has been opposition to the government's stand on these points that has prompted Japanese, often spurred on by the Left, to take to the streets in organized protest."

In Okinawa, however, the problem remains. U.S. military installations still occupy some 15 percent of the total land area. Opposition among Okinawans to U.S. bases is adamant, Blaker said, even though overt displays of local resentment are becoming less frequent.

Opposition to the presence of nuclear weapons in Japan remains a potentially explosive political issue, the more so because Japan has pledged firmer adherence to the "Three Nuclear Principles" that affirm that Japan will "not use, manufacture, or allow nuclear weapons" in Japan. Up to the present time, only the final "principle" has caused headaches, arising from claims that U.S. warships capable of being armed with nuclear weapons actually have had such weapons aboard when visiting Japan. Japan's position on the status of U.S. nuclear weapons remains ambiguous and even ironic, Blaker observed: "On the one hand, it wants a firmer nuclear shield; and yet, on the other hand, it balks at, or only tacitly accepts, the entry into its territory of the weapons that impart credibility to that commitment."

The third and thorniest issue, Blaker stated, is the nature and extent of Japan's contribution to regional security. In Japan, discussion of this question primarily has been with the geographical boundaries of the region. Japan would be obligated to render support to U.S. military action in those reaches under the terms of the treaty. However, this perimeter never has been drawn formally with much precision. At various times it has encompassed mainland China, Quemoy and Matsu, Taiwan, Siberia, and the Kurile Islands. And although Vietnam was never included, Tokyo nonetheless gave assistance to U.S. forces during the Vietnam War.

Korean Security

The ambiguity in defining the outermost lines of Japan's regional security commitment is far less apparent with regard to Japan's closest neighbor, Korea. Acknowledging the fact that any conflict on the Korean peninsula might place Japan in an extremely delicate situation, Japanese defense officials and the "hawks" in the LDP oppose a withdrawal of U.S. forces from Korea. This was made very clear in 1977 when the United States announced a phased withdrawal of its troops from South Korea. In the event of a U.S. withdrawal, Japan (in a defense white paper published in 1977) stated that it would accept the move on several conditions: that the number of ground troops removed be kept to a minimum, that the process take place incrementally, and that Tokyo be kept informed of decisions beforehand. President Carter, of course, did not proceed with the withdrawal, but the concern expressed by Japanese officials over the announcement at least indicated a greater sensitivity to potential instability in Northeast Asia.

Conclusion

Nonetheless, Dr. Blaker conjectured that it is unlikely Japan will abandon its decision to rearm gradually and to reject both the nuclear option and the acquisition of clearly offensive conventional weaponry, even in the event of a conflict in Korea. It is the Japanese preoccupation with their vulnerable economic and strategic position, Blaker said, that makes a military future seem suicidal. In all likelihood, he said, Japan will be content to remain a "porcupine," militarily, for some time to come.

4

ANTI HEGEMONISM AND U.S.-PRC-JAPANESE SECURITY COOPERATION

Dal Choong Kim, *Yonsei University*

The concept of U.S.-PRC-Japan triangular cooperation has been developed as a strategy to counter Soviet expansionism in East Asia. From the Chinese point of view, the Soviet Union clearly is trying to edge out the United States, isolate Japan, encircle the PRC, dominate East Asia, and so achieve hegemony in the region. The United States also believes that the Soviet Union is a threat that must be checked. To a lesser degree, Japan also considers the USSR a threat to its security. Of the three nations opposing the Soviet Union, the PRC apparently feels the most threatened by the USSR.

Having identified the Soviet Union as the principal enemy as early as 1971, China set about establishing a united front with Japan and the United States. China signaled its support for a continuing U.S. military presence in East Asia and encouraged Japan to increase its military capability. To a certain extent, even China's "four modernizations" serve the interests of this united front against the Soviet Union. This is because China views close economic cooperation with the West not only as a way to enhance its military capability, but also as a device to keep these countries politically close to China.

Beijing's World View, Hegemonism, and the United Front

China's foreign policy strategy has always been explained and by Beijing's leaders in terms of their world view. As their world view has altered in response to a changing international environment, their foreign policy has accordingly been modified.

After the founding of the People's Republic of China in 1949, the Chinese saw the world divided into two hostile camps, namely, the socialist camp led by the Soviet Union and the capitalist or imperialist camp led by the United States. With the outbreak of the Korean War in June 1950, China began to perceive the United States not only as a political and ideological threat, but also as a real military and security threat. The decision by President Truman to order the Seventh Fleet to resume patrol of the Taiwan strait was taken by the Communist Chinese as a drastic reversal of the previous official U.S. position of noninvolvement in China's civil war. In response to the U.S. policy of containing China, Beijing concluded a military alliance with the Soviet Union. In the meantime, China courted newly independent and developing nations and called for a revolutionary armed struggle against the United States.

The outbreak of the Sino-Soviet dispute in 1960 forced the Chinese leaders to again change their world view. Believing the Soviets to be colluding with the United States after Khrushchev agreed to dismantle missile bases in Cuba in late October 1962, the Chinese adopted a united front strategy against the Soviet revisionists and the U.S. imperialists. Japan and those Western nations that were undergoing rapid economic growth were designated by China as belonging to the "second intermediate zone."

In January 1964, the term "hegemony" was used for the first time in an editorial of *People's Daily*. In it, the writer charged that U.S. hegemonic foreign policy was the main reason for friction within the capitalist camp. At the beginning of the 1970s, China thought the United States was declining as a world power while Soviet expansionism was growing. To describe the relationship between the two major powers and the "small and medium" countries, Zhou Enlai introduced the concept of "super-power hegemonism" toward the end of 1970. At this time, he pointed out that the international situation was increasingly favorable to the small and medium countries. Since then, China has identified itself as one of the small and medium countries and has pledged that it will never seek to become a superpower.

In 1971, Beijing launched several attacks on superpower hegemonism, first in the U.N. General Assembly in November 1971, then in December 1971, when Zhou Enlai directly attacked the Soviet Union, declaring that social-imperialism has always been unscrupulous in carrying out aggression and expansion and contending for world hegemony. At this point, the Chinese introduced the "theory of three worlds" in which the superpowers make up the first world; Japan, Europe, and Canada the second; and China and the Asian, African, and Latin American countries the third. Of the two superpowers, the Soviet Union was seen as the principal enemy, Dal-Choong Kim said, because it is a hegemonist power bent on subjecting the entire world while the United States is on the defensive.

To counter this Soviet threat, China signed the Shanghai Communiqué with the United States in February 1972. In the communiqué, both parties pledged that "neither should seek hegemony in the Asian-Pacific region and each is opposed to any effort by any other country or group of countries to establish such hegemony." To reinforce China's commitment to oppose hegemony, the antihegemony concept was included in the party constitution in 1973 and then in the state constitution in 1975.

Antihegemonism in Sino-Japanese Relations

During the 1950s, Japan was left out of China's major strategic considerations because Japan was regarded as a client of the United States. However, following the stagnancy of the great leap forward, the poor harvests for three consecutive years after 1959, and the withdrawal of Soviet advisers in 1960, China began to consider Japan an important economic force which it could emulate. As a result, Sino-Japanese trade expanded fairly rapidly during the first half of the 1960s.

Toward the end of the 1960s, China began to regard Japan not only as an important economic force in Asia, but also as a military power that might be brought into a united front against the Soviet Union. This followed the announcement of the Nixon doctrine in July 1969 and the subsequent speculation that the U.S. withdrawal of its forces would be offset by Japan assuming the defense burden hitherto borne by the United States. Therefore, both to prevent Japanese remilitarization and to contain the growth of Soviet influence in East and Southeast Asia, China began to actively use the concept of antihegemonism in its foreign policy.

With the signing of the joint Zhou-Tanaka joint statement in September 1972, China checked possible Japanese expansionism with the inclusion of an antihegemony clause in the statement. "From this time on," Dal-Choong Kim said, "they [China] appeared to concentrate their diplomatic efforts on forming the U.S.-PRC-Japan triangular united front struggle against Soviet hegemonism." Chinese intentions were plainly stated when Zhou Enlai said that "China welcomes the reinforcement of Japanese military strength as a potential counterweight to Soviet aggression."

Thus, with the Soviet Union identified as the main enemy, the stage was set for the establishment of diplomatic relations between China and the United States in December 1978. From the Chinese point of view, the signing of the Treaty of Peace and Friendship between China and Japan on August 12, 1978 was a significant diplomatic victory because it was the first time that China had succeeded in stipulating the antihegemony principle in a legally-binding international agreement. All that was left was to normalize Sino-American relations and complete the triangle.

Antihegemonism in Sino-American Relations

Since the signing of the Sino-American Shanghai Communiqué in February 1972, there have been different opinions about Beijing's decision on rapprochement with Washington. Some think that the relationship will not last past the time when the ideological differences between China and the Soviet Union have been eliminated or China has become strong enough to effectively counter the Soviet threat. But other observers believe that Sino-American rapprochement goes beyond Chinese concern for their national security. In their opinion, rapprochement was also a means for China to enhance its international status and influence. As evidence, they point to Zhou Enlai's report to the Communist Party in December 1971 when he said that "at this stage, it [was] necessary to take advantage of the contradictions between the U.S. and the USSR and to magnify it." Therefore, Dal-Choong Kim said, China sought to separate the Soviet Union and the United States and form a Beijing-centered united front against the Soviet Union.

This was the first goal mapped out by the Chinese in pursuing rapprochement with the United States. The second goal was to have the United States accept the three preconditions for normalization of relations: U.S. withdrawal of forces from Taiwan, the severing of U.S. diplomatic relations with Taiwan, and the abrogation of the U.S. mutual defense treaty with Taiwan. The third goal was to enhance Sino-American bilateral socioeconomic cooperation.

To facilitate reaching an agreement with the U.S., China agreed in the Shanghai Communiqué to observe the principles of peaceful coexistence in regulating international disputes and to renouce the use and threat of force, particularly with regard to Taiwan. Moreover, China agreed to establish a diplomatic liaison office in Washington while the Nationalist government of Taiwan still maintained an embassy in the United States. This was a major compromise on the part of Beijing, Professor Kim said. These demands and compromises then enforced the basis for normalization of relations between China and the United States effective since January 1979.

Conclusion

The United States, Chinese, and Japanese strategic triangle of cooperation, which has emerged as a result of China's seeking an antihegemonic united stand against the Soviet Union, has the potential, Professor Kim said, to destabilize the balance of power that has existed for almost three decades among the four powers and thereby greatly increase the possibility of conflict in the region. Apprehensive about what it has called "a military alliance" and "an Asian NATO," the Soviet Union, Kim warned, may go beyond building up its influence in the region as it has done in Vietnam and encourage North Korea to initiate an attack on the South in order to drive a wedge between the Peoples Republic of China and the United States. "In the event of an open conflict on the Korean peninsula, China, bound by a treaty to defend North Korea, could not stay aloof and let the Soviet Union reassert its dominant influence over North Korea," Kim said. And if Kim Il-sung believed it was his last chance to use military force to reunify the peninsula in view of the widening political, economic, military gap between the North and the South, then, warned Kim, the possibility of renewed military conflict in the Korean peninsula—instigated and supported by the Soviet Union— is even greater.

If Moscow continues its expansionist policy, then the United States will respond and pursue greater military cooperation with China. But it should do so cautiously, Professor Kim warned. In the 1980s, he said, it is necessary "to maintain an equilibrium of power in the region, thus preventing any single power from establishing a dominant position." Only in this way can another military conflict on the peninsula be avoided. To safeguard that peace and to maintain stability in the whole region, Kim concluded, the United States should strengthen its overall defense capability; enhance its forward military posture in the region; consolidate the U.S.-Japan alliance; reactivate the four-nation balance of power in place of the emerging bipolar confrontation between the Soviet Union and the strategic triangle composed of the United States the PRC, and Japan; and, lastly, maintain its security commitments to its traditional Asian allies. Unless the United States does this, Dal-Choong Kim said, it might find itself in a position where its role as a stabilizer may be forfeited.

5

THE SINO-SOVIET CONFLICT AND ITS IMPACT ON THE KOREAN PENINSULA

Chang-Yoon Choi, *National Defense College*
(in absentia)

The Sino-Soviet dispute is one of the crucial factors that affects peace and stability on the Korean peninsula. Deeply suspicious of each other's motives, both powers are involved in a zero-sum game in which Chinese losses are profitable to the Soviets, while the Soviets' losses are beneficial to China. In this paper, Chang-Yoon Choi outlined the situation in Korea in the context of the Sino-Soviet dispute and explained what that would mean in terms of a new outbreak of hostilities on the peninsula, the continued presence of U.S forces in South Korea, and the possibility of reunification of the two Koreas.

Strategic Value of the Korean Peninsula

Historically, the Korean peninsula has been strategically important to both the Russians and the Chinese. It is, said Chang-Yoon Choi, the "geostrategic locus" where the interests of both powers collided. Therefore, because of its strategic importance, whoever controlled the Korean peninsula also controlled all of Northeast Asia.

In accordance with their traditional view of Korea, Annam, Outer Mongolia, and the countries in the Himalayas as being within their outer spheres of influence, the Chinese often have referred to Korea as "the lips protecting the teeth of China," or as a wall protecting the industrial and resource centers of Manchuria and Beijing. For these reasons, China has viewed a dominant position in Korea as vital to its security and interests. With the Sino-Soviet dispute, Korea assumes even greater importance.

Korea is no less important to the Soviet Union, especially as it is adjacent to the Maritime Provinces of Siberia. "Vladivostok, the long-time home port of the Soviet Pacific Fleet, is so close to Korea," Chang-Yoon Choi pointed out, "that the Soviet Navy must be attentive to what is happening on the Korean peninsula." An increase of Soviet influence in the area would not only give the fleet security and enable it to maneuver more freely, but it would also allow the Soviet Union to impose a tactical check on China and at the same time use Korea as a jumping off point for further expansion. A loss of Soviet influence, on the other hand, would incur consequences that are unacceptable to the USSR.

Given the tensions created by the Sino-Soviet dispute, Chinese concern with the dangers posed by an increase in Soviet influence in East Asia is not unreasonable. In the event of a breakout of hostilities, the Soviets would then be in a position to threaten Manchuria on three sides. At the same time, the USSR could prevent the United States from coming to the assistance of China and deter a Chinese drive into the Maritime Provinces by threatening both the rear and the front flanks of Chinese forces. With control of the Yellow Sea and the Sea of Japan, the Soviets could secure the sea lines of communications and effect a complete blockade of the Chinese coast and the Chinese North Sea Fleet.

If the Chinese secured control of North Korea however, then the Chinese could easily control the Yellow Sea and eliminate the threat of a Soviet attack along her coast. Moreover, the Chinese could advance toward the Sea of Japan and threaten the Soviet Pacific Fleet; they could also, attack areas in the Soviet Maritime Provinces and detroy, block, or threaten the lines of communication for Soviet Far Eastern forces in the rear. Chinese control of North Korea would also form a buffer zone, allowing China to avoid direct confrontation with U.S. forces in South Korea.

Sino-Soviet Conflict and a New Korean War

As the arms race between the two Koreas intensifies, the possibility of a new war cannot be ruled out. Kim Il-sung, Chang Yoon Choi said, is irrational and unpredictable and perfectly capable of setting off a war in the peninsula. In such an event, both the Soviet Union and China could either restrain or encourage Pyongyang,

Choi said, depending on how they perceived their national interests in terms of Sino-Soviet conflict.

The Soviet Position. It is possible that the Soviets might encourage the North to attack the South. In supporting the North, the Soviets perhaps would be able to break up the anti-Soviet coalition made up of Japan, the United States, and the People's Republic of China, as the PRC would then be forced to help North Korea and so bring itself into confrontation with the United States. In addition, the Soviets might support an attack by the North in the belief that their influence in North Korea would increase—as happened in Vietnam during and after the war— and so gain a strategic advantage not only over China but also over Japan and the United States.

However, upon closer examination, the Soviet position is probably ambivalent, if not somewhat negative. One reason for this is that Moscow probably would not wish to devote the major resources necessary to support a conflict in Korea, especially if the North was defeated, as this would be a major blow to Soviet credibility. A second reason why the Soviets might be reluctant to support Pyongyong, Choi said, is that they would want to avoid another confrontation with the Chinese. Third, a unified Korea would be less readily controllable than the North is now, since a unified Korea would be in an even stronger position to play off Moscow against Peking to its own advantage. And fourth, a new war in Korea endorsed by the Soviet Union would hasten the anti-Soviet coalition among the United States, China, and Japan.

The Chinese Position. For similar reasons, the Chinese are also reluctant to support an offensive by the North. First, China does not wish to devote the major resources necessary to support a conflict in Korea, given its primary concern with carrying out modernization. Second, the Chinese fear that the Soviets would seize the opportunity to extend their influence in North Korea, as happened in Vietnam. Third, the Chinese are apprehensive that an outbreak of hostilities on the Korean peninsula would result in a massive rearmament of Japan. And, finally, the Chinese are concerned about the potential for independent action on the part of a unified, highly nationalistic Korea, as well as about Korea leaning more heavily toward the Soviet Union to obtain the industrial, technical, and economic assistance that China is unable to provide. The restraint exercised by the Chinese in April 1975 when Kim Il-sung visited Peking, looking for support for military action against South Korea, and again in 1976 when the tree-cutting incident in Panmunjon took place, indicates, said Choi, that the Chinese are reluctant to encourage Pyongyang to unify Korea by force.

The Soviet Union, China, and the U.S. Forces in South Korea

The United States has played a major role in preserving peace and stability on the Korean peninsula. Its military presence, Choi said, has helped bolster South Korea's capacity to deal with North Korea's threat of aggression. It has deterred North Korea from launching an attack against the South, and it has created a more stable equilibrium among the major powers in Northeast Asia. This is why, Choi said, North Korea's consistent position has been that the U.S forces should withdraw promptly and totally from South Korea. The Soviet and Chinese positions, however, have been less clear and precise.

The Soviet Position. The U.S. military presence in South Korea, Choi said, must loom large in the Soviet perspective in view of its confrontation with China, because the U.S. presence presents both opportunities and obstacles to Soviet policymakers. It is an obstacle, he said, because the U.S. forces in South Korea are positioned only a few hundred miles from vital Soviet installations, closer to the homeland than any other U.S. combat formation, thus preventing Soviet pressure from bearing too hard on Japan or China and blocking a Soviet advance in East Asia. However, the U.S military presence in South Korea also restrains an increasingly independent North Korea and so saves the Soviets from being drawn into the conflict in order to balance Chinese support. "There is little evidence," Choi said, "that the Soviet Union considers U.S. forces in South Korea a significant threat to their interests under present circumstances." Indeed, an analysis of Soviet writing on the subject reveals relatively mild Soviet concern over the U.S. presence in the South. Certainly, it is milder than that expressed by Pyongyang. Every now and then, the Soviets have called for the "total and immediate" withdrawal of U.S. forces, but most statements, Choi pointed out, appeared on ceremonial occasions, such as the founding day observance of the North Korean government or the anniversary of the signing of the mutual defense treaty with Pyongyang. Hence, the Soviets see the U.S. presence as conducive to their interests, as well as an obstacle.

The Chinese Position. The ambivalence of the Soviets toward U.S. forces stationed in South Korea is not shared by the Chinese, as the United States does not pose the same security threat to China as does the Soviet Union. In fact, Choi observed, "it may actually be to China's political and military advantage to encourage the American military presence in South Korea and other parts of East Asia, except for the forces in Taiwan, which the Chinese consider a wholly internal affair." The reason for this is that, first, the Chinese regard the United States as a counterbalance to the Soviet Union, which helps to deter Soviet expansion in Asia, reduces the changes of a Sino-Soviet war, and discourages the Soviet Union from using its nuclear weapons against China. In this regard, the U.S. military presence is a necessary sign to the Soviets of U.S. determination to defend its interests in Asia. Moreover, the U.S. forces in South Korea serve to maintain the status quo in North Korea, South Korea, and Japan, thus preventing a fundamental change in the regional military balance that would occur if South Korea acquired nuclear weapons or Japan rearmed substantially.

Chinese support for a continuing U.S. military presence, Choi warned should not be construed as a sign that Peking no longer supports North Korea in its struggle with the South. Rather, China's abandonment of its uncompromising position in the mid-1970s has been in its own interests, because an outbrek of a new war on the peninsula "would gravely undermine China's efforts to strengthen its position relative to the Soviet Union by cultivating its relations with the United States and Japan and by carrying out its four 'modernizations.' "

Sino-Soviet Conflict and Korea's Unification Problem

Both the Soviets and the Chinese publicily support the eventual reunification of the two Koreas. In an analysis of Soviet writings between 1975 and 1978, the frequency of statements in support of North Korea's unification policy ranked second among the 29 Korean-related topics. In such statements, the Soviets depict themselves as the only true and reliable friend of the Korean people on the question of unification. The Chinese, the Soviets charge, do not really want Korean unification. In private, though, Moscow is less optimistic. Believing that peaceful unification is unlikely in the foreseeable future, they have proposed that the problem should be handled along the lines of the "German model"—that is, the great powers should recognize both Koreas as separate states. It is perhaps for these reasons that the Soviet Union opened unofficial contacts with South Korea in 1973 and has been supportive of a peaceful solution to the extent that Moscow, said Choi, has cooperated with

U.S. efforts to reduce tension and promote stability on the Korean peninsula.

Unlike the Soviets, the Chinese do not acknowledge either in private or in official conversations that Korea is likely to remain divided for a long time. Yet there is little evidence, either in China's behavior or in its public statements, according to Choi, that it expects unification within the foreseeable future. That it would probably take a long time was hinted at by Deng Xiaoping on his visit to Japan in October 1978, when he said that reunification of Korea could take as long as a thousand years. Perhaps because of this, China quietly has been supportive of U.S. efforts to reduce tension and to promote stability on the peninsula.

In practical terms, the Chinese have been open to compromise. The agreement reached by Zhou Enlai and Secretary of State Henry Kissinger in October 1973 over the resolution proposing the abolition of the UN Commission while still retaining the UN command in South Korea is an example. The willingness to support a tripartite conference involving the United States and North and South Korea, as reported by U.S. Senators Jacob Javits, Frank Church, and Joseph Biden after their meeting with Deng Xiaoping in April 1980 is another example. The expressed willingness by Peking to take part in the 1988 Olympic games in Seoul and to engage in nongovernmental economic and personal exchanges with South Korea is yet another example of softening of Chinese attitudes. In attempting to explain this shift in policy, Choi suggested that, partly, it was because China wanted to preserve the status quo and partly because an improvement in relations with South Korea would give China access to technology on terms more favorable than either the United States or Japan could offer.

In response, the South Korean government also has shown some signs of flexibility toward China. At a news conference in Washington in February 1981, Chun Doo Hwan stated that "if the People's Republic of China is a friend of the United States, I think I can extend the logic and say a friend of a friend is less of a threat to us than the other power that you have mentioned." In April of 1981, he further clarified South Korea's position when he said:

> We are as a matter of principle in favor of exchanges of goods and people with countries that do not agree with us ideologically, provided that those countries do not take hostile action against us. But I do not believe it will be easy for us to improve these relations rapidly. The U.S. could help us, for example,

by helping to persuade China to engage in an exchange of goods, to recognize the Republic of Korea and help the Republic of Korea become a member of the United Nations. Then the U.S. could recognize the existence of North Korea.

The recently reported willingness by the South Korean government to permit commercial aircraft to fly between Tokyo and Peking over South Korean airspace is another message of flexibility toward China.

Conclusion

Despite the relaxation in the stance of the different parties involved, the hostility between North and South Korea creates one of the most volatile and dangerous situations in Northeast Asia. But whether or not a new war on the peninsula will break out largely depends on the outcome of the Sino-Soviet dispute.

With regard to the attitude of China and the Soviet Union toward supporting a North Korean attack, both have indicated some support for the reunification of the two Koreas by force, but both have also displayed negative and ambivalent positions to protect or strengthen their own national interests.

For the same reasons, the Soviets and the Chinese have differed in their positions on the presence of U.S. forces in South Korea. The Soviets, Choi said, are equivocal, as they see the U.S. presence as an obstacle to further expansion, but at the same time believe those forces to be a helpful check on both North Korea and China. China, for its part, Choi said, seems to favor, or at least tolerate, the presence of the U.S forces in South Korea because they are a check on the Soviet Union, Japan, and North and South Korea, and thereby contribute to the stability of Northeast Asia.

The reluctance of the Soviets and the Chinese to upset the status quo in Korea also is shown in their positions on the unification of the two Koreas. Stressing the need for peaceful rather than forceful unification, both the Soviets and Chinese, Choi said, are engaged in "watchful waiting." In the interim, the Soviet Union seems to be pursuing a "two Koreas" policy at nongovernmental levels, while China is also showing some degree of flexibility toward South Korea while publicly defending North Korea's "one Korea" solution. But one important thing has to be borne in mind, Choi warned, and that is this:

> While the policies of the Soviet Union and China toward the Korean peninsula and their policy objectives can account for a

substantial amount of the variation in the situation in Korea, North Korea's decisions and interactions between the two Koreas themselves are of much more significance to the Korean problem.

6

SINO-SOVIET RELATIONS IN THE 1980s AS A FACTOR IN NORTHEAST ASIAN SECURITY

Thomas W. Robinson, *Georgetown University;*
Adjunct Fellow, CSIS

The Sino-Soviet dispute has been a factor for stability in Northeast Asia for nearly 25 years. While Moscow and Beijing have been locked in a struggle to determine the ideological correctness of their respective positions, South Korea, Japan, and the United States have had to worry less about conflict with the two Communist giants, singly or together, or with North Korea. As a result, both Japan and South Korea could concentrate on economic development by spending less on defense, while the United States became more deeply involved in Asia. Even after China emerged from the Cultural Revolution, there was further strengthening of regional security with rapprochement of China and the United States and Japan and China. Continued U.S.-Japanese and U.S.-Korean security cooperation, Soviet diplomatic bungling, and the self-induced isolation of North Korea further guaranteed the peace

The Future of Sino-Soviet Relations

Until recently, the central working assumption in all capitals, said Robinson, remained the continuation of irreconcilable differences between the People's Republic of China and the Soviet Union. But now, he said, many of the constants of Northeast Asian security are beginning to change. In particular, the U.S. and its Asian allies can no longer count on prolonged out-and-out Sino-Soviet enmity. In the short-and medium-term, such developments as the probable drawing apart of the United States and China, the possible rearmament of Japan, the heightened potential for conflict in Korea, Southeast Asia and in the Taiwan Strait, and the continued Soviet buildup in the region may outweigh changes in Sino-Soviet relations. "Nonetheless, the comparative importance of the Soviet-Chinese factor is so high" Robinson noted, that even a relatively small improvement in the short term could well exert a disproportionate effect on the overall situation."

Until the late 1980s, China will be unable to move too far from the United States, or to repel a Soviet attack without U.S. assistance; nevertheless, China will seek to be equidistant from Moscow and Washington. Movement in this direction can already be seen in the deliberate cooling of diplomatic relations between Beijing and Washington, the declind in trade between the two countries, and the abandoning of discussions on developing military ties. It can also be seen in the upturn in trade between China and the Soviet Union, in the welcoming of Soviet delegations to China, in the dispatch of various groups to the Soviet Union, and in the recent Chinese response to Soviet diplomatic overtures concerning the border question and security talks.

From a strategic point of view, the Soviets are in a dilemma about their China policy. On the one hand, they occupy a very strong short-term position wherein they could now destroy most Chinese cities and occupy significant portions of Chinese territory. Yet, on the other hand, a decade of Chinese economic growth and military modernization would counterbalance much of this initial Soviet advantage, set the stage for Chinese replacement of Soviet influence in Asia, and provide Beijing with the capability to inflict unacceptable population and even territorial losses on the Soviet Union. If China were to cooperate with the West, this would be perceived by the Soviets as an even greater threat to their national security. For these reasons, the Soviets have every incentive to compromise on issues that presently separate the USSR and China.

In China, various internal factors mitigate in favor of improvement in Sino-Soviet relations. As Chinese politics began to tilt back toward the Left in 1981, the Deng Xiaoping faction has come under increasing criticism not only over his compromising stance on Taiwan, but also over his policy toward the United States. Concerned with becoming too closely integrated with a capitalist economy, China therefore began to draw back from plans emphasizing vastly expanded foreign trade and the importation of Western capital and looked back to the Soviet Union as a source of capital goods and funds.

In view of the fact that Sino-Soviet relations are likely to improve steadily during the 1980s, it is probable, Robinson said, that the United States would be drawn back into the region—especially if Sino-Soviet rapprochement is accompanied by progressive deterioration in Sino-American relations. However, there is a certain danger in U.S. forces then being stretched beyond their means. In the event of crises in the Persian Gulf or the Caribbean, Robinson warned, severe risks would have to be taken in Asia and, in extremes, some Asian allies would have to be temporarily abandoned. In the long term, then, the United States would have to decide whether or not it had the resources and willpower necessary to continue to play the global game effectively. In all likelihood, Robinson said, the United States will conclude that it cannot confront China and the Soviet Union alone. Under such circumstances the United States will have no other option than to pressure its allies, such as Japan, to increase their material inputs.

Whether and to what extent Tokyo would respond to this U.S. pressure would depend on the state of Japanese internal politics and on Japan's econcomic relations with the United States. However, if Japan began to feel threatened by both the Soviet Union and China, then her relations with them would decline and closer relations with the United States would be restored. And if Japan rearmed in consonance with U.S.-Japanese plans, then the military balance in Northeast Asia would be maintained. But if Japan rearmed far beyond the requirements of the situation, that balance would be greatly upset. Consequently, China and the Soviet Union might be pushed together faster and further than would otherwise be the case.

On the Korean peninsula, the Sino-Soviet rapprochement could trigger a new Korean war. Viewing the resolution of the dispute between China and the Soviet Union as a threat to their autonomy, North Korea could well launch an attack against the South to fulfill Kim's final wish or unite the nation behind Kim's successor. With closer ties between the USSR and China, Robinson speculated, joint Soviet-Chinese pressure could be brought to bear on North Korea to refrain from initiating an attack. In that case, the rapprochement would lead to an actual decrease in the threat to Seoul. And if the United States decided to strengthen its commitment in the region, the result could be an all around enhancement of South Korean security. "The overall level of tensions would be higher between the Communist states and the Free World," said Robinson, "but there would be areas of calm—eyes within the storm system."

The First Scenario

When changes in Sino-Soviet relations are considered in the context of other likely developments in Northeast Asia, several scenarios emerge.

The first scenario is a projection of current trends. In it, the position of the United States vis-à-vis the Soviet Union continues to slip, while the confidence of the Chinese in U.S. abilities to deter Soviet expansionism will also decline. As a result, both Western Europe and Japan would drift apart from the United States and into compromising positions and policies toward the Soviet Union as U.S. leadership within the Western alliance is increasingly called into question. In the meantime, China would pursue steady economic development at home and a middle-of-the-road line in its foreign policy. In this scenario, it is not unlikely that the United States would be drawn out of Asia into a conflict in the Persian Gulf or the Caribbean, thus providing China, Vietnam, and North Korea with excellent opportunities to solve by force the Taiwan, Indochinese, and Korean "problems."

What is the probable influence on Sino-Soviet relations of these possible developments? According to Robinson, two courses of action are possible. The first is that a Sino-Soviet détente would be achieved fairly rapidly as Beijing and Moscow resolve their differences without having to take the United States into account. The second course predicts a slowing down in Sino-Soviet détente as each competes for influence in Asia. Ironically, this renewed Sino-Soviet rivalry would facilitate U.S. diplomatic and military initiatives in the region as the smaller Asian nations again seek the assistance and protection of the United States.

In the economic sphere, Sino-Soviet détente could well lead to a greater willingness by European and Asian leaders to work together to solve their economic problems. In such an atmosphere, the United States might also show an increased willingness to compromise its economic differences with Europe, Japan, and the oil exporting states, and to form a more equitable partnership with these countries thereby helping solve many of the problems in the global economy.

On balance, then, a Sino-Soviet defente that gave rise to increasing economic rivalry between the two Communist giants and to greater Western unity would not be cause for undue alarm. In the event of a conflict with either China or the Soviet Union, the picture, of course, would change. Western unity no doubt would be strengthened, but it would be accompanied by the rapid restoration of the Cold War and the threat of a global war.

The Second Scenario

In the second scenario, there is an overall improvement in the condition of the United States and its allies. With a Sino-Soviet détente, the Soviet Union would be forced to soften their conditions for settlement with the Chinese to offset the formation of a global entente to which they could not adequately respond. On the other hand, the Chinese, armed with U.S. assurances for their security but nonetheless concerned with losing Taiwan, would also press for an improvement in Sino-Soviet relations.

The Third Scenario

In the third scenario, the United States and its allies would weaken economically, politically, and militarily at an accelerated pace. With Western unity shattered, Europe and Japan would progressively adopt policies of appeasement toward the Soviet Union, while the United States would spin itself into an isolationist cocoon. Alarmed at the turn of events, the Chinese would first reestablish close relations with the Soviet Union and then work closely with the Soviets in the hope of pursuing their plans for regional expansion, causing a decisive and permanent shift in the global balance in favor of socialiam. This is hardly a pretty scenario, Robinson said, but it is not entirely unrealistic, even on the basis of currently visible trends.

Conclusion

From the three scenarios it can be seen that Sino-Soviet futures are relatively nondependent of the character of the external environment. When these external factors are ignored, it seems that Sino-Soviet détente will occur. Yet it will not be necessarily bad for regional security. When these external factors are taken into account, some scenarios are worse for regional security then others, even though all would accelerate Sino-Soviet détente. Obviously, détente under conditions of a rapid restrengthening of the United States would be preferable to one where the United States or its allies are economically and militarily weak.

As for Korea, Robinson believes that neither the North nor the South can significantly affect Sino-Soviet détente. Kim Il-sung or his successor may decide to launch an attack aginst the South. In response, China and the Soviet union might present a united front to Pyongyang against the attack or they might support North Korea as part of a coordinated offensive against U.S. allies. The latter case would take place where U.S power had significantly declined.

Like the North, South Korea's policy options are limited. Beyond continuing along the present path of political stability and rapid economic growth, with an attendant increase in domestic military strength and willingness to engage in trade and negotations with its Communist neighbors, South Korea can do little else. Still, it could, of course, decide to produce its own nuclear weapons, to expand its trade and political ties, and to reconcile its differences with Japan. With regard to the first of these options, the production of nuclear weapons by South Korea hardly seems possible in the early 1980s, said Robinson, especially as it would be enormously counterproductive to ties with the United States. The second and third options, he said, should be pursued anyway.

III

Two Koreas in a Changing Environment

7

POLITICAL SUCCESSION IN NORTH KOREA

Suk-Ryul Yu, *IFANS*

In his paper, Yu explored the character of the North Korean regime, giving special attention to the question of political succession. Yu defined North Korea as a totalitarian Communist state, characterized by the unlimited and unrestrained power of its rulers and the suppression of all forms of autonomous opposition. What distinguishes the North Korean regime, Yu asserted, is the bizarre attempt being made by North Korean dictator Kim Il-sung to establish a family dynasty by making his 40-year-old son, Kim Jong-il, his political heir.

Generally speaking dynastic succession is precluded in Communist regimes by the ruler's intolerance of rival sources of power. Should Kim Il-sung bring about a dynastic succession during his lifetime, the aging dictator will have turned Marxist doctrine upside down with a vengenance and will have succeeded in doing what no other Communist leader has ever even attempted. If the current North Korean political situation continues for the next several years, North Korea will probably become the first Communist country under hereditary rule, Yu contended.

The success of Kim Il-sung's efforts to effect hereditary succession, according to Yu, depends upon a variety of factors not the least of which is a demonstrated lack of leadership qualities on the part of Kim Jong-il. In the first place, Yu contended, Kim Jong-il lacks the required personal appeal and stature for the job of national leader. He does not have his father's unrivaled prestige with which to enforce unity among the top leaders. He was not involved in the anti-Japanese efforts during the struggle for independence and did not render any distinguished service to his country after the Korean liberation in 1945. Further, he lacks the military experience of his father, who fought as a partisan, and he did not serve during the Korean War.

Furthermore, according to Yu, Kim Jong-il lacks experience and skill in dealing with other Communist nations including the USSR and China—both of whom have issued strong criticism of possible hereditary succession within North Korea. The younger Kim was designated as Kim Il-sung's successor only because of the strong backing of his father. His political base is still narrowly confined to the operational wing of the military and to a "new breed" of younger cadres, according to the North Korean sources analyzed by Dr. Yu.

On the issue of Kim Jong-il's leadership potential, Yu noted also that there is a definite lack of charisma—a problem that the elder Kim is attempting to rectify through an idolization drive. This lack of charisma is compounded by the fact that Kim Jong-il lacks his own ideology—his own version of "Kim Il-sungism" (the worship of Kim Il-sung). Unquestionably, the numerous institutes and study groups of "Kim Il-sungism" (including "Juche" ideology) organized at home and abroad have assisted that leader in his efforts to solicit pro-Pyongyang groups and North Korean sympathizers.

These factors will no doubt hinder Kim Jong-il's efforts to acquire and maintain control amid the instability consequent upon his father's death. His present situation and future prospects are further dimmed, Yu noted, by the existence of major external opposition to hereditary succession in North Korea. Citing the 1970 *Dictionary of Political Terminology* published by the Democratic People's Republic of Korea's (DPRK's) Academy of Social Science, Yu noted that the concept of hereditary succession is ideologically anathema to Communist regimes. In that work, hereditary succession is described as "a reactionary custom of exploitative societies," (an entry that was absent in the later 1973 edition). As Yu indicated, no other Communist country has acknowledged, much less endorsed, Kim Jong-il's rise as heir-apparent, though both the Soviet Union and the PRC have made certain concessions in diplomatic protocol to the possibility of Kim Jong-il's succession (such as toasting the health of Kim the younger at diplomatic gatherings). Although the USSR and the PRC might avoid any active opposition to Kim Il-sung's blatent king-making, their negative feelings about hereditary succession could give a strategic advantage to those opposed to the Junior Kim when the struggle for power eventually erupts.

Even more significant for the prospects of hereditary succession are the sources of internal resistance, including the ruling elites, technocrats and specialists, and opposition both within the Kim family and among the general public.

Yu asserted that within the ruling elite one can distinguish two alienated forces: one within the Korean Workers Party (KWP) and the other within the military. The first includes individuals opposed to the concept of hereditary succession and to the takeover by Kim Jong-il in particular. Many aged party leaders so-inclined, including Kim Jong-ju, Ryu Jang-shik, and Kim Dong-gyu, have been demoted or removed from power altogether, thus strengthening the hand of the younger party radicals, said to be a major source of Kim Jong-il's support.

The military, noted Yu, has also proven to be a center of opposition to the younger Kim's rise to power. Outright resistance surfaced when junior military officers made an attempt on Kim Jong-il's life in 1977. Open resistance by the military seems, however, to have decreased considerably. The military commanders of divisions, regiments, and battalions have been continuously replaced with younger officers. Most generals in North Korea are presently in their fifty's and sixty's, certain to be replaced in the near future by Kim Jong-il's Mangyongdae Revolutionary Academy alumni now in their forty's.

A second major source of internal opposition to hereditary succession can be found among technocrats and other elite groups generated as a by-product of industrialization. Such groups tend to view things pragmatically and thus oppose a single-minded commitment to "revolutionary lines" and the junior Kim's adventurist policies.

Further, Yu noted, the question of hereditary succession depends in large part on the struggle for primacy within the ruling family. Tracing the vicissitudes of the various family contenders for power, Yu described how Kim Young-ju, Kim Il-sung's younger brother, was appointed director of the Organization and Guidance Department of the KWP Central Committee, which oversaw all party personnel matters in 1966. He was also appointed a member of the KWP Politburo and Secretariat. In 1970 he ranked sixth in North Korea's power structure. By taking advantage of his powerful position, he consolidated his power base in the party. But in 1973 he was replaced by his nephew Kim Jong-il and was demoted from sixth to thirteenth place. In 1974 he was again demoted and made one of several insignificant deputy premiers. The KWP figures personally associated with him were also automatically demoted and disappeared.

From 1975 to 1978, struggle for power between Kim Jong-il on one side, and his stepmother and his uncle on the other, became intensified. Eventually, however, Kim Jong-il won, while Kim Yong-ju and Kim Il-sung's wife, Kim Song-ae, were removed or demoted from their positions of power along with their followers. But struggle for power between them is not over yet. It is known that there is bad blood between Kim Song-ae, Kim Il-song's present wife, and Kim Jong-il. When Kim Jong-il came to power as designated successor, Kim Song-ae was demoted from sixty-seventh on the list of the 1970 KWP Central Committee members to one hundred and fifth on the 1980 list of the same committee because he idolized his deceased mother, Kim Jong-suk.

Kim Jong-il repeatedly emphasizes that his dead mother was a better revolutionary than Kim Song-ae, a better wife to this father, and better First Lady for the country. Upon the commencement of the "Drive to follow the Example of Mother Kim Jong-suk" in June 1976, Kim Song-ae was deprived of her honorific title, "Madame." She and her husband have since been referred to as "President Kim and his wife." In addition, it is reported that Kim Jong-il purposely reinstated on kun-level three party secretaries who had been dismissed by Kim Song-ae in June 1974, and Kim Jong-il intentionally removed his stepmother's image from the commemorative picture of the New Year of 1974. But Kim Song-ae is reportedly a powerful political personality in her own right, and she has firm faith in her husband's policies.

Kim Il-sung married his present wife, Kim Song-ae, in 1950. He has five children (two sons and three daughters) by his second marriage. Kim Song-ae's first son, Pyong-il, is now old enough (28 years of age) to take part in the struggle for power. He is reported to be ambitious, far better in character, brighter, and more capable than Kim Jong-il. Kim Pyong-il is reported to have been sent to the East German University for a while, but now he is in the military service and building up his power base in the military. His relationship with Kim Jong-il appears to be tense and stormy. There is a growing possibility of a ruthless struggle for power between them. It is apparent that Kim Pyong-il's younger brother, Song-il (21 years of age), will be another strong political enemy for Kim Jong-il as he grows up.

In his discussion about attitudes among the general public, Yu pointed out that the North Korean people are reputedly classified into three major ideological categories: core, oscillating, and hostile. The hostile class comprises "untamable heretics," ranging from counterrevolutionary elements to relatives of defectors to South

Korea and expatriates from Japan. The class is deemed to be a "dangerous element," which opposes the North Korean revolutionary policies and is discontented with the designation of Kim Jong-il as heir-apparent. It is reported that about 105 thousand North Koreans are being held in custody as "ideological criminals" at eight different concentration camps in the North. It seems that most of the silent populace, as well as the hostile class in North Korea, is discontented with the arrogant activities of the Three-Revolution Squads that seek to provide legitimacy to the hereditary succession. The squad's armed conflicts with the party members and others at Shinuiju in November 1981 attest to the general public's growing discontent with the dynastic succession.

What are the future prospects for North Korea's political development in general, and for Kim Jong-il's succession in particular? While not overlooking the plethora of variables influencing both developments, Yu posited that the time of Kim Il-sung's death will be most decisive. If Kim Il-sung dies within five years, Yu asserted, it is doubtful that the younger Kim could successfully maintain his rule. In the wake of the older Kim's death, a small collective leadership, with Kim Jong-il the "first among equals," will probably emerge to shoulder the mantle of rule. The shape and content of such a collective leadership cannot be predicted. What is sure, noted Yu, is the inevitable confrontation of Kim Jong-il and his ideologues with a coalition of military personnel seeking rapid reform and technocrats advocating modernization.

Yu forsees two possible outcomes of the cut-throat struggle for power. If Kim Jong-il's forces win the battle against the opposition, the junior Kim will attempt to remove the anti-Kim forces completely by taking advantage of the strong military backup under the leadership of Oh Jin-u and Oh Guk-ryol. He will also take a harder militant line to control the North Korean people tightly. Kim Jong-il will command the entire country, it is anticipated, while Oh Jin-u and Oh Guk-ryol control the party and the military. Lim Chun-chu will be a possible replacement for Prime Minister Lee Jong-ok and he may be in charge of government affairs, ideology, and unification issues. If the allied forces of the military and technocrats win the battle, a new collective leadership will emerge, removing all Kim's forces from the positions of powers. During the struggle, or even in the short period after winning the battle, there is some possibility that the allied forces will use Kim Pyong-il, Kim Song-ae's first son, as a figurehead. It is evident that they will attempt to gain support from the general public by choosing a soft-line based on China's pragmatic model for modernization.

The time factor in the succession question is so important to its outcome, Yu contended, that if Kim Il-sung's death does not occur for ten more years, Kim Jong-il will surely succeed his father. This period will give the son time to learn from his father. He will not fail to consolidate and strengthen his position in order eventually to restore one-man rule. He will gradually eliminate all potential opponents including the old guard within the country and bring in younger men more dependent on himself. He will also attempt to infuse new blood into the top leadership. Accordingly, Kim Il-sung's ideology and policy continue under Kim Jong-il's leadership.

In concluding, Yu put forth several proposals for a strategy designed to establish a durable peace and achieve reunification of the Korean peninsula in the period prior to the consolidation of Kim Jong-il's new regime.

1. Because there is a great possibility of another war during this period, the ROK first should beef-up its defense capability. The United States should continue to show North Korea its firm determination to resist any use of force against the ROK and the U.S. government should be fully prepared for North Korea's blitzkrieg type of warfare.
2. The Western countries, including the United States and Japan, should not attempt to improve relations with North Korea. North Korea, under the pressure of internal instability, will not be able to change its policy even though the Western contacts aim to weaken North Korea's aggressiveness. The contacts, instead, will give a unilateral strategic advantage to the Kim forces. It is desirable, therefore, that the Western countries should not contact North Korea during this period. The ROK and the United States should work together to persuade Japan to follow that line.
3. South Korea and her allies should let North Korea know that the most dangerous threat to North Korea's own security is not the United States and South Korea, but the Soviet Union, as witnessed in the Soviet invasion of Afghanistan and the Vietnamese invasion of Cambodia. There are possibilities that Moscow could move into Pyongyang to dominate North Korea, taking advantage of the unstable internal situation. The United States should carefully watch the Soviet moves during this period.
4. It is advisable that the ROK should repeatedly urge North

Korea to accept President Chun's proposal for "Democratic Reunification through National Reconciliation." Pyongyang will not accept the proposal, but it will be placed in a diplomatic dilemma.
5. The ROK should devise a proper measure to let the North Koreans know of President Chun's proposal and to encourage them to democratize Kim Jong-il's new dictatorial regime, hoping that the measure gives strategic advantage to Kim's opposition. It is evident that the consolidation of Kim Jong-il's power will be the worst outcome for South Korea and her allies.

Yu maintained that in a period after the consolidation of Kim Jong-il's new regime, the following should be considered:
1. Although the possibility of war will be somewhat decreased, there should be a concerted effort by Seoul and its allies to force Kim Jong-il to wake up from his "false hopes" and "illusions" about unification by force. At the same time, the United States should demonstrate to Pyongyang that there is no chance for North Korea to drive a wedge between Seoul and Washington.
2. It is anticipated that Kim Jong-il may initiate several unification proposals for the sake of bolstering his political legitimacy. Thus, it will be a good time for the ROK to institutionalize peace in inter-Korean relations by strategically taking advantage of Kim's unification proposals.
3. It is desirable that the United States and Japan, in close coordination with South Korea, should contact Pyongyang on a limited basis. Through such contacts, they should seek to institutionalize a durable peace on the Korean Peninsula.

In the event of a new "anti-Kim" collective leadership, Yu advised that the best course of action would involve the following:
1. U.S. troops should continue to be stationed in South Korea, despite a balanced military situation on the peninsula. South Korea may be able to advance arms reduction negotiations and a nonaggression treaty between the South and North as a result.
2. The ROK and her allies should encourage Pyongyang to resume a direct inter-Korean dialogue as a means of providing a genuine starting point for resolving the problems between the two Koreas.
3. The United States could encourage its allies to help open North Korea's door to the West so that North Korea would become subject to outside influence and, thereby, might weaken its aggressiveness.

4. The U.S. effort to encourage its allies to improve their relations with North Korea should be done without provoking Moscow and without stimulating an imprudent expansion of Japanese trade, which may encourage North Korea's aggressiveness. If Moscow comes to the conclusion that North Korea is lining up along with China, Japan, and the United States in an anti-Soviet coalition, it may be tempted to invade Pyongyang to put North Korea under Moscow's control.
5. The ROK should become an object of emulation for North Korea by further promoting public welfare and democracy.

8

NORTH KOREA AFTER KIM IL-SUNG

Ralph Clough, *The Asia Society*

Much has been written about the decision of Kim Il-sung to make his son, Kim Jong-il, his successor. Should he succeed, a rift in the top leadership may develop and relations with the Soviet Union and China could become strained, according to Ralph Clough. Nevertheless, the potential impact of the succession on North Korea should not be overstressed. This is because many things will remain the same or change only slowly, regardless of who succeeds Kim Il-sung and how that person comes to power.

Basic Factors

Foremost among the factors to be considered by the new leader are those relating to the geographic and demographic situation of North Korea. Surrounded by three powerful neighbors, Korea, throughout its long history, has been subjected to invasion and occupation of part or all of its territory by foreign armies. To a certain extent, these factors have influenced Kim Il-sung's outlook. Because of this, Kim has remained wary of both China and the Soviet Union and has resisted taking sides in the Sino-Soviet dispute, despite Soviet pressure in the early 1960s to do so. In fact, Kim secured his position in the early 1950s by purging pro-Chinese and pro-Soviet factions from the Korean Workers Party. Thus, as a result of North Korea's proximity to the three major powers in the region and the political situation on the Korean peninsula itself, in which the North faces an economically superior and more heavily populated South backed by U.S. forces, any successor to Kim Il-sung will have to form his policies along similar lines. The methods he adopts may be different, Clough pointed out, but the problems will remain the same. That is, Kim's successor still will have to deal with the perceived threat from the South, the North will continue to depend on its allies for its security, and the fear of being dominated by those allies will remain.

Trends Since 1970

Economic, diplomatic, and strategic trends since 1970 have altered the position of the North in relation to the South, and cannot be ignored by any successor to Kim Il-sung. In the economic sphere, the Communist system itself, Clough explained, was the basic cause of slow economic growth in the 1970s in the North. Lacking a market mechanism, investment has been diverted out of the most productive areas, heavy industry has been stressed at the expense of light industry, and quantity is given predominance over quality. As a result, low labor productivity is an endemic problem. The gradual ossification of the hierarchial social structure of North Korea, the long periods of time spent in political indoctrination sessions, and the aging, outdated machinery in the factories compound the problem of low productivity. This is in marked contrast to South Korea, which has experienced rapid economic growth.

In an attempt to break out of its cocoon of isolation and close the gap between the North and the South, Kim turned toward Japan and various West European countries in the early 1970s to obtain factories and machinery. But his efforts did not succeed. Hit by bad harvests in 1972, which required using valuable foreign exchange to buy Australian wheat, and affected by a drop in the prices of its export products at the time when the price of oil sharply increased, North Korea found itself in great difficulties. Unable to pay back the loans extended to it by Japan and the West European countries, North Korea lost its access to foreign credits. Sales of military equipment, especially to Iran, have probably become a significant foreign exchange earner for North Korea, Clough said, but North Korea's large military industry absorbs much investment capital and labor that could be turned to more productive uses and contribute more to economic growth.

The unabated military buildup of North Korea during the 1970s kept tension high between the two North Koreas, despite the hopeful beginning in 1971–1972 when direct dialogue was begun for the first time. An agreement was reached on principles for reunification in July 1972, but differences in interpretation cropped up almost immediately and the talks between the North and South stalled and then broke off in 1973. Commenting on the failure to reach agreement in 1973, Clough said that both parties seemed more interested in establishing a strong propaganda position in the talks than in probing each other's position to determine where reciprocal concessions might lead to agreement. Since then, both sides have strived to outdo the other in putting forward new proposals for the reunification of Korea and in gaining the support of foreign countries, almost as if they were engaged in a deadly serious popularity contest, Clough said. Up until 1970, the South led in establishing diplomatic relations around the world. But during the 1970s, the North made important diplomatic gains. In the main, South Korea has stressed economic relations and has appealed to those countries with pragmatic leaders, whereas the relations of the North have been more political. The latter has therefore attracted those Third World leaders whose approach to international affairs is highly ideological.

The dogmatic approach of the North is reflected in its opposition to cross-recognition, in which each Korea would maintain diplomatic relations with the United States, Japan, China, and the Soviet Union. While itself seeking contacts with South Korea's principal supporters, the United States and Japan, North Korea has been opposed to China and the Soviet Union establishing similar ties with the South. In response, the U.S. government has declined official talks with North Korea unless South Korea is also a full participant or unless the Soviet Union or China is willing to have talks with South Korea comparable to those the United States would hold with the North.

North Korea After Kim

Elements of Continuity

North Korea almost certainly will remain a Communist state after the death of Kim Il-sung for, unlike Eastern European countries such as Hungary, Czechoslovakia, and Poland where elements of capitalism have long been embedded and which still have numerous connections with the West, North Korea has no significant traditional ties to the West.

Up to the present time, North Korea has been politically stable because Kim has been able to maintain extensive and tight control over the population and has also been able to bring about an improvement in the standard of living, but this stability may not continue after Kim's death. Lacking the skill at political infighting, Kim's successor may find himself embroiled in a power struggle at the top. In addition, he will be confronted not only with the problem of reunification with South Korea, but also with a growing and rigid bureaucracy at home. And should the Sino-Soviet dispute continue, then the new ruler will also face the dilemma of how to balance North Korea's relations with its two Communist allies so as to best serve the North's national interest and preserve its independence.

The Succession

Kim Il-sung's decision to appoint Kim Jong-il his successor stems partly from the fact that North Korea, like other Communist countries, lacks an accepted institutionalized method of choosing a new leader, and partly from the fact that Kim Il-sung is unwilling to leave the succession to the outcome of a power struggle among the surviving senior leaders. Having seen how the new leadership in China and the Soviet Union have veered sharply from the path charted by the original revolutionary leader, Kim Il-sung chose his son to maintain the system he has established in North Korea and to pursue meticulously the policies that he has designed.

To justify what is in fact hereditary succession, a system they once condemned as a "reactionary custom of exploitive societies," North Korea now has described it as "a scientific solution to the question of inheriting the leader's revolutionary cause," and as "a key to successfully inheriting and completing the leader's revolutionary cause." However, reluctant perhaps to have their plan for hereditary succession exposed to criticism outside North Korea, especially by other Communist countries, the North Korean media referred obscurely to Kim Jong-il throughout the 1970s as "the party center." It was only after the Sixth Congress of the Korean Workers Party in October 1980, which named him to the fourth position in the 5-member presidium of the politburo, second in the 10-member secretariat, and third in the 19-member military commission (only he and his father hold concurrent positions in all three), that Kim Jong-il's name began to appear frequently in North Korean publications. Describing him in such terminology as "the brilliant son of communism who is a paragon of loyalty" and the "great Kimilsungist," his role is defined as a policy aide to his father in charge of drawing up policies on behalf of the party and the government in every domain, including diplomacy and national defense.

Despite the disapproval of China and the Soviet Union, it is unlikely that Kim Il-sung will be dissuaded from pursuing his succession plans. Korean tradition, Clough said, favors acceptance of the succession among the North Korean people. The long-lived Yi dynasty, Clough pointed out, effectively followed the principle of hereditary succession, usually by the eldest son of the king, to minimize struggles for power at the summit. Nevertheless, the timing of Kim Jong-il's rise to the top will be important, as he needs time to gain needed experience in high level positions and to consolidate his power at each step by placing loyal supporters in key positions and eliminating those of doubtful loyalty. In this context, the appointment of O Kuk-yol also of the Mangyongdae Revolutionary Academy, as chief of general staff in 1979, was significant, as is the fact that in recent months Kim Jong-il has appeared frequently in the company of Defense Minister O Chin-u. The succession also has to be timed properly so that Kim Jong-il himself doesn't become a threat to Kim Il-sung.

If Kim Jong-il remains a filial son and turns out to be a skillfull politician capable of lining up his supporters and eliminating his opponents, then the succession will proceed as planned. But it is also possible that the younger Kim may become a puppet of what Clough termed "more skillful operators" who use him as a front, exploiting the Kim Il-sung myth for their own purposes. Alternatively, he may be brushed aside by the elite in North Korea in much the same way as Khrushchev broke with the Stalinist tradition and as Deng Xiaoping has done with Maoism in China.

Choices for Kim Il-sung's Successors

Regardless of who succeeds Kim Il-sung, the fundamental problem that will face any new North Korean leader is how to create a more dynamic society to compete more effectively with the remarkable dynamism of South Korea. And herein, said Clough, lies the dilemma facing the North Korean leadership. Having told the people that they already "live in a paradise on earth," the new leaders, Clough said, "must decide whether to cling to the old fictions that have assured political stability for 30 years, but have also caused increasing rigidity and sluggishness in the system, or to strike out boldly along new lines, taking big risks to gain big rewards."

If they want to compete with the South, then the North must not only loosen centralized controls, introduce material incentives and a greater reliance on market forces, but it must also, like Hungary and Yugoslavia, open its doors to a massive influx of information and technology from the West. The choices left to North Korea are only two—to perpetuate the "hermit kingdom" philosophy, glorify Juche, and maintain a Kim family personality cult and fall even further behind in modernizing the nation, or to accept the need for either gradual or rapid change that will bring it more in tune with the modern world. The latter choice, said Clough, is the most probable. "When this happens," he said, "the probability will rise dramatically for a North-South dialogue aimed at stabilizing a state of peaceful coexistence between the two Koreas and cross-recognition of both by the big powers."

9

THE OUTLOOK OF THE FIFTH REPUBLIC OF KOREA: A STUDY OF THE SOCIALIZATION PROCESS OF THE NEW POLITICAL LEADERS

Brigadier General Tong Hui Lee, *Korean Military Academy*

With the tragic end of the Yushin regime at the close of the 1970s, the Korean people again faced hardship and national crisis. The so-called October 26th incident (the assassination of President Park Chung Hee) was the culmination of a series of national crises. In the political sphere, the monopoly and rigidity of power precipitated the collapse of national consensus. Stagflation and structural distortion, both produced by rapid growth-oriented policies, afflicted the economy. Compounding these problems was a discernible dissolution of the traditional value system under the weight of uncritically accepted foreign mores.

The year following the incident presented the interim government with the most severe national crisis since the liberation of the country from Japanese colonial rule, according to General Lee. An ominous period spent waiting for the leading powers to reconstruct a new political and social order ended in the advent of the Fifth Republic. The foundation of that republic, asserted General Lee, was enough in itself to change the anxiety and chaos of these dark days into hope and order.

General Lee's optimism derives from his belief that the rise of the Fifth Republic represents the revolutionary change of generations in leadership structure. According to Lee, the advent of the new leadership signifies departure not only from the Fourth Republic generation, but also from many fundamental contradictions that have perennially plagued Korea's nation-building efforts. President Chun Doo Hwan has boldly removed the old power structures and laid the groundwork for the leaders of the new generation to enter and advance as the new elite.

In discussing the nature of this "new generation," General Lee ascribed to it the following characteristics: a clear political ideology, a legalistic and rational comprehension of governmental processes, and a highly developed sense of morality and civic virtue.

Elaborating on the first point, Lee posited the discernible existence of a clear political ideology. President Chun is the first holder of that office to have been educated in, and to receive a degree from, the Korean educational system. Nurtured within this system, he has thus grown with the concept of national identification and matured as an idealistic person, according to General Lee.

The emergence of a more legalistic and rational perception of government, the second characteristic of the new leadership, was attributed by General Lee to the rise of a Western-educated elite to positions of authority. Members of the administration and of the National Assembly are technocrats able to determine national policies rationally on the basis of specialized knowledge and experience. General Lee pointed out that in the area of politics, the standards of education for the members of the Assembly have improved. Collectively, these factors will facilitate the employment of more effective and efficient methods to achieve rational and reasonable policy goals.

The third of these attributes, a highly elevated sense of morality, is of equal importance. General Lee asserted that the new leaders are very moral people. Their shared experience in the Korean Military Academy (KMA) has imbued the leaders of the Fifth Republic with common ethical values. As KMA cadets, they were subject to an honor system, and to the cadet creed, which states, in part, "I will choose righteousness in defiance of indolence and dishonor." Further, their development was shaped by the KMA's educational objectives: instilling conscious military professionalism, arousing a consciousness of mission, and enhancing strict anti-Communist attitudes to ensure the continued survival of democracy. The fact that the ruling elite of the Fifth Republic has had these same goals as their basic objectives for over three decades portends their extension from the classroom to the political arena, according to Lee.

These three attributes will stand the new leaders in good stead as they confront very formidable and pressing national tasks. General Lee enumerated these tasks, which involve the following areas of concentration: 1) Nationalism, which embodies the ideal of one people in one state charting their own course; 2) Modernization and balanced development between technology and social well-being; 3) "Koreanization" through anti-Communism; 4) Unification through peaceful means; and 5) Democratization through increased public participation and peaceful transfer of power.

General Lee defined the first of these tasks, nationalism, as a mental state that facilitates the congruence of national spirit and political substance. Nationalism, founded on the recognition of the nation as an ideal form of political organization, engenders the social contract whereby a people overtly or tacitly consent to be governed and to assist in the development and continued independence of the nation.

In Korea, Lee pointed out, for the past 30 years the movement toward nationalization based on the concept of self-reliance has promoted social development and social order and has enhanced the stature of the nation in the world arena. The desire for independence and self reliance is complemented by a growing cosmopolitanism. The more liberal travel and education policies adopted by the Fifth Republic will, General Lee believes, expand the collective consciousness of the people, thereby strengthening the fabric of nationalism.

In elaborating on the task of modernization, General Lee described it as perhaps the most important objective of nation-building efforts. In the early post-World War II period, Korea's five-year economic development plan produced an annual average growth rate of over 10 percent. Unfortunately such rapid growth brought about severe structural problems, while also perpetuating the unequal distribution of wealth among social classes. Over the last decade, the latter problem has diminished somewhat in the face of a burgeoning middle class. In a 1980 survey conducted by *Chosun Daily*, and cited by Lee, about 70 percent of respondents answered that they belonged to the middle class (upper middle: 11.4 percent; middle: 39.5 percent; lower middle: 27.7 percent.) Moreover, 70 percent replied that they are enjoying comfortable lives, and 47 percent pointed out that their standard of living has greatly improved since the 1960s.

Despite such optimism, the fact remains that the Korean economy is in a serious crisis today because of the worldwide recession and the structural problems that have accumulated over the last 20 years. Issues of balanced growth, social welfare, and income distribution are being raised. Increasingly subject to criticism are the low wage/

rapid growth oriented policies, and the export-oriented trade practices that prevailed in the past. The Fifth Republic, Lee explained, has adopted the establishment of social welfare as a national ideology. As a first step, it ended the government's monopoly of power, rationalized the organizations overseeing economic development, and undertook various social development programs. The goal of the leadership is efficient and balanced economic development—a prerequisite to accomplishing the other four nation-building tasks.

The third of these tasks, "Koreanization," involves coming to terms with the sometimes forceful impact neighboring areas have had on Korean culture and with the intrusion of Western values accompanying industrialization and modernization. The Fifth Republic, according to General Lee, has done much to promote the synthesis of "oriental thought and Western technology" in its educational reform and cultural enhancement programs.

As Lee pointed out, the most detrimental restraining factor in the national development of Korea is the reality of a nation divided. The unification of the Korean peninsula is a key precondition for stability and peace and for the prosperity of democracy in that area.

The Fifth Republic has, Lee asserted, demonstrated absolute dedication to peaceful unification, employing both bilateral and multilaterial contacts. In January 1982, 20 proposals for trial projects were announced. They included proposals for mutual visits, for bilateral discussions, and for a democratic unification scheme. Lee pointed out that while such efforts must be mindful of national security requirements, there should be no abuse of the security issue to impede democratization.

Democratization, the final nation-building task, has been greatly facilitated by the Fifth Republic's constitution, which seeks to pluralize political parties, encourage popular participation in politics, and activate judicial and legislative organs. Institutionalization of peaceful political transition procedures merits special notice, Lee suggested.

In his conclusion, General Lee noted the interdependence of these five tasks. Growth of the social organism is curtailed by the deterioration or stagnation of any one of its several parts. General Lee noted that, in the past, overemphasis on economic growth or single-minded dedication to reunification, for instance, contributed to dictatorial practices. Lee stressed that a country with an able and far-sighted electorate, confident in the ability of its law-makers, can accomplish the five nation-building tasks by interaction and cooperation. The leadership of the Fifth Republic, aptly described by

General Lee, appears to be ready and willing to meet these challenges, to continually improve the quality of life within the country, and to stand as able allies alongside all sovereign powers everywhere who share similar ideals.

10

OUTLOOK FOR THE FIFTH REPUBLIC IN THE 1980s: INTERNATIONAL LAW IMPLICATIONS OF "ECONOMIC DIPLOMACY"

Nam-Yearl Chai, *Columbus College*

This year, 1982, marks the centennial of the U.S.-Korea Treaty of Friendship, Commerce, and Navigation—the treaty that literally as well as figuratively opened the door of the Korean kingdom, allowing it to gain firsthand knowledge of the practice of Western international law. In those early days, the international transactions were limited in both scope and variety.

Today, the scope and depth of transactions involving international law for the Fifth Republic is far beyond the imagination of the people who lived 100 years ago. With the Fifth Five-Year Economic Development Plan, the Korean leadership is committed to what is popularly termed "economic diplomacy." The 1982 export target is said to be nearly $25 billion. More than 3,000 General Trading Companies (GTCs) are conducting export business.

Together with these export activities, the Chun administration, Chai said, is sparing no effort to attract advanced foreign industrial technology by making the terms of contracts very appealing. Numerous technical license agreements have already been entered into with foreign firms and governments. In the past decade, there have been nearly 2,000 such agreements—many of them having been concluded during the present administration.

While technology transfer is being effected rapidly, numerous joint ventures are also on the rise, both primary joint ventures—the so-called 50-50 rule—and split-equity joint ventures. That is not all.

In the 1980s, an increasing number of Korean industries will go multinational; already, they are taking part in coal mining in Alaska, TV manufacturing in Alabama, jointly running an electronics plant in Tennessee, and there is even a joint venture in corn farming, to mention just a few. Furthermore, more than 100 thousand Korean workers are said to be working in the Middle East, Chai noted.

What does all this mean to the Fifth Republic from the standpoint of international law? From the legal viewpoint, it will mean that the government will be called upon, more and more, to intercede on behalf of Korean business communities and nationals abroad. Transnational litigations involving doctrines of state responsiblity, state immunity, exhaustion of local remedy, *force majeure,* and *rebus sic stantibus* (or changed circumstances) will increase in frequency and intensity.

The Fifth Republic will do well, Chai warned, to exercise diligence in making certain that every major transnational contract contains an arbitration clause as a dispute settlement mechanism, so as to obviate costly litigation. Special care must be taken also to ensure a maximum utilization of the services of the Korean Arbitration Association.

What is even more serious, as the Fifth Republic finds its competitive edge in the world market further diminishing—due not only to keen competition from the less developed nations in labor-intensive industry sectors, but also to mounting protectionism from the developed nations—is that the policymakers in government will be tempted to resort to extra-legal measures of a dubious as well as a devious nature.

Already, Chai observed, allegations are made of Korea's complicity in the piracy of technology. According to the May 1982 issue of *Far Eastern Economic Review,* Dow Chemical charged that a Korean firm purchased from a third party a stolen formula for one of Dow's products. In essence, Dow contended that the firm in question knowingly acquired the stolen formula.

The same magazine mentioned another such case—this one has the tone of a comic-opera script. A certain foreign firm that set up a distributorship in Korea received a purchase order for an advanced piece of machinery. However, much to the chagrin of the foreign company, the Korean government withheld permission for the machinery to be brought into the country. The reason given was that another Korean company was said to have the production capability. Further investigation resulted in the discovery of a reasonable facsimile of the machine on the premises of a lumber mill.

The best inducement for increased foreign investment in Korea in the 1980s and beyond, Chai cautioned, is not through crafty manipulation of international law to one's advantage, rather, it is through the availability of fair and equitable legal procedures, including legal remedies. In transnational business transactions, nothing equals predictability, certainty, and orderliness. And international law, in spite of its manifold shortcomings, is said to be best suited for providing such a modality.

In a sense, it is encouraging, Chai said, to note that the current administration is bending backward to accommodate foreign investors. A 100 percent equity ownership is often granted to some foreign investment, especially in non-Japanese derived investment. Such magnanimous concessions will more than adequately offset some shortcomings that still need to be overcome in the areas of patent laws and tax court decisions.

Whenever feasible, the Fifth Republic in the 1980s is urged to make full use of the arbitration services of the International Center for Settlement of Investment Disputes, a body affilitated with the World Bank. Parenthetically, the government in the 1980s should show its renewed resolve to adhere to the UN Convention on the Recognition and Enforcement of Foreign Arbitration Awards. In addition, the present administration is urged to accede to the Hague Convention on Legal Document Certification.

If the Fifth Republic in the 1980s made a modest contribution toward bringing those international trade practices employed in pursuance of "economic diplomacy" in line with the norms of international law, Chai said, the benefits accrued from such a reputation will not be confined only to the southern half of the Korean peninsula. Located in a strategic corner of the Pacific Basin, the Fifth Republic of South Korea in the 1980s will be in an enviable position as a catalyst that could lead the way toward a closer partnership among other Pacific Basic countries.

11

TWO KOREAS IN THE GLOBAL CONTEXT

Kie-Pyung Oh, *Sogang University*

The two Koreas were created by the big powers after World War II as a result of ignorance and military expediency. As the strategic nexus to the four major powers—the United States, China, the Soviet Union, and Japan—Korea plays a crucial role in maintaining the peace and stability in the region and in the rest of the world. However, so long as Korea remains divided, the danger of conflict in the area will be greatly increased as the big powers strive to exert their influence on the peninsula. But this is not to be unexpected, as the two Koreas owe their current status mainly to the four major powers. Both North and South Korea derive their political systems from the Soviet Union and the United States respectively—and owe their economic existence to either China or the United States.

In this paper, the major issues pending between the two Koreas will be clarified, and the influence of external forces on these issues will be examined. The three major issues are legitimacy, security, and unification. However, although unification is the central concern of both Koreas and cannot be separated from the other issues, it will not be considered in depth here.

Some Clarifications

There is disagreement concerning the most adequate definition of security. In this discussion, security can be defined as all national defense devices directed against external threat. This includes the military capability to deter the threats from the other side and other security measures that are integral parts of international arrangements provided to assure the safety of each polity. In the case of the Republic of Korea, such assurances are provided by the United

States and the United Nations, while the People's Republic of China and the Soviet Union provide similar guarantees of security to North Korea. Because of this involvement of outside powers in Korean affairs, "there is," Kie-Pyung Oh said, "no reason for a concept of absolute security which assumes total conquest of the other side by military means." For this reason, the security of both Koreas requires skillful diplomacy in order to gain the support of other nations, particularly the big powers.

The efforts by both Koreas to win the recognition of other nations is also prompted by the need to enhance their legitimacy in the world community. The passing of UN resolution 195 (III) recognized the ROK as the sole legitimate government in the Korean peninsula and so justified ROK's adoption of the Halstein doctrine in establishing diplomatic relations. But in reality, the legitimacy of the South has been secured by its close ties with the United States. Similarly, the legitimacy of the North has been secured only through the support of China and the Soviet Union. As a result, both sides have strived to expand their respective diplomatic networks, especially after the brief thaw between the North and the South in the early 1970s, when Seoul modified its claim to be the sole legitimate government in the Korean peninsula. As of May 1982, the two Koreas were nearly equal in the number of countries with which they had diplomatic relations. The South was recognized by 116 states and the North by 101, while 64 states recognized both Koreas. "This indicates," said Kie-Pyung Oh, "that there is a split legitimacy on the Korean peninsula."

Environment: Patterns of Major Power Relations

The pattern of major power relations in Northeast Asia in the 1980s will be a function of shifting relations among the six pairs of two-nation "dyads" of the United States and USSR, the United States and Japan, China and the United States, China and Japan, Japan and the USSR, and the USSR and China. During the present decade, slight change may occur in the relationship between the United States, China, and Japan, but it is unlikely that any fundamental and drastic changes will take place in the international environment and the configuration of power among the major powers. This is not to say that there will be an absence of conflict in the region. As Kie-Pyung Oh pointed out, there are abundant sources of conflict in Northeast Asia—for example, there are territorial disputes among China, the Soviet Union, and Japan; and between

China and Japan. And then there are the two Koreas, each uneasily trying to adjust to the shifting policies of the major nations. The changing role of the United States in Asia, the quarrel between the United States and China over Taiwan, and the strained relations between Japan and the United States have all added to the uncertainty and fear of instability in the region.

According to Kie-Pyung Oh, one of the major destabilizing factors has been the Soviet Union. In response to the Soviet military buildup in the region, the United States sought rapproachment with China. In turn, the Soviet Union accelerated its buildup to offset this new threat. The enhanced vigilance of the Soviet Union in the region is ascribed primarily to the Sino-Soviet dispute. Yet, said Kie-Pyung Oh, this phenomena could be better explained as the aftermath or dysfunction of the U.S.-Soviet detente that existed in the 1970s. It could, of course, be said that the Soviet buildup has been exaggerated by U.S. military strategists in an attempt to secure sufficient funds from Congress for defense, but it would be more likely that the Soviet military threat led the United States and its allies in Asia, including the ROK, to engage in what Professor Oh termed "the vicious circle of competitive military buildup."

A second cause of instability has been the new détente between the United States and China. Originally believing that détente with the PRC would be a significant check on North Korea, the United States has since been compelled to reevaluate its relationship with China as it has become more apparent that China is more concerned with its "Four Modernizations" and "Soviet hegemonism," that it is about Korea. The consequent attempt by the United States to achieve strategic independence from the Sino-Soviet dispute, together with its decision to proceed with arms sales to Taiwan, has further added to tensions in the area.

The third destabilizing factor derives from U.S. efforts to strengthen its alliance system. During the Cold War era of the 1950s and 1960s, defense alliances with the United States were based on the premise that the United States enjoyed military superiority over the Soviet Union. At that time, the perceived superiority of the United States was sufficient to deter an attack from whatever source on an ally of the United States. Now, however, with parity between the United States and the Soviet Union, "the term military alliance," Kie-Pyung Oh said, "has come to have any realistic meaning only when it is based on actual capability." This means that U.S. allies will now have to buildup their forces significantly. And with this, Kie-Pyung Oh warns, comes the possibility of local nuclear warfare, as tactical nuclear weapons are used in place of conventional weapons simply by the decision of a military strategist or field commander. Eventually, such a war, Kie-Pyung Oh predicted, would escalate to a global nuclear war. However, for the moment, this is unlikely to occur, he said, because the existing cooperative mood among the three major powers will continue for a considerable period of time.

The possible rapprochement between China and the Soviet Union could also destabilize the region. Such rapprochement may take place if China decides to take a course independent of the United States and the Soviet Union, but to a great extent, it will depend on the rate and depth of adjustment of U.S. strategy in Northeast Asia. When it is excessive, abrupt, and unilateral, then the probability of rapprochement will be heightened. In such an eventuality, the United States will have to overhaul its entire global strategy. This is because an outbreak of hostilities in the Korean peninsula in the wake of a Sino-Soviet rapprochement would have a direct bearing on Sino-American detente, as both China and the United States have mutual security treaties with North and South Korea respectively. For the moment, though, both countries are more interested in preserving the status quo in the Korean Peninsula than in any changes which would enable the Soviets to increase their influence and perhaps disrupt China's modernization.

Competition in trade and raw materials, friction over mutual investment and military bases, and general U.S. credibility problems will be sources of conflict in U.S.-Japanese relations. To a certain extent, they will add to the uncertainty in the region, but they are unlikely to be major factors for destabilization. In fact, Professor Oh noted, Japan appears to be a "coprogramer" of U.S. foreign policy in the region.

The normalization of Sino-Japanese relations has made it clear that Japan also would prefer stability based on the territorial status quo in the Korean peninsula. The reason for this is that if hostilities broke out in Korea, not only would Japan have to decide on whether or not to permit U.S. forces the use of their bases in Japan and so run the risk of Communist retaliation, but a new Korean war also would directly threaten Japan's own security.

For different reasons, the Soviet Union also seeks to maintain the status quo in the Korean peninsula. This is clear from the fact that in the 1970s, the Soviet Union sought contact with South Korea and refused to support North Korea's claim to be the sole sovereign government in Korea. At the same time, despite the rhetoric, there appears to be considerable doubt, Kie-Pyung Oh suggested, about the extent of genuine, active Soviet support for the North's unification policy. As for Kim Il-sung's succession plans, the Soviets will probably pay lip-service to his intentions.

Thus, it appears the major powers will endeavor to maintain the status quo in Korea to avoid any deep involvement in a possible conflict, to lessen their risks and military expenditure, and to prevent the two Koreas from being unified by a power hostile to them. This being the case, the only alternative open to the two Koreas, said Kie-Pyung Oh, is for them to resolve their problems peacefully through negotiations. At first, there should be direct negotiations between the North and South on the matters of unification and simultaneous admission to the UN; and then, later, talks may take place between the United States and North Korea, as long as they include South Korea.

State of Negotiations Between the Two Koreas

Given the desire by the major powers to maintain the status quo, military force and revolutionary violence cannot be used to solve the problems in Korea. Therefore, negotiation is essential and indispensable if they are to be settled by peaceful means. To begin with, the existence of two Koreas must be accepted as a fact of life if meaningful steps toward a peaceful settlement are to be taken.

At the present time, it seems unlikely that a solution will emerge in the foreseeable future, despite the promising developments of July 1972 when a joint communiqué was issued announcing agreement on a number of basic principles concerning the unification of the two Koreas. Begun in September 1971 after President Richard Nixon's visit to Peking, the negotiations ended abruptly in August 1973 owing to the diametrically opposite positions taken by the two sides. From the outset, the North insisted on an immediate far-reaching politico-military settlement, while the South sought a gradual resolution of outstanding problems. In line with this approach, President Park of South Korea announced on June 23, 1973 a new open door policy toward "nonhostile" Communist states based on the principle of reciprocity and equality. Going even further, he announced that South Korea would not object to joining the United Nations together with North Korea. In response, Pyongyang issued a proposal for the formation of a confederation of North and South Korea and reiterated its five-point proposal for unification.

The resulting impasse has not yet been broken. Stating that negotiations with the South would only perpetuate the division of Korea, the North has refused to resume talks. For the same reason, Pyongyang has opposed separate membership or simultaneous admission of both Koreas to the United Nations. But this is not the real reason, according to Kie-Pyung Oh. North Korea also has opposed simultaneous entry of the two Koreas into the UN as the North would therefore not be obliged to abide by the UN charter and so would be in a better position to justify its use of force against the South as a purely internal matter in which no other nation could interfere.

Prospect of a U.S.-North Korea Negotiation

Periodically, North Korea has attempted to improve its relations with the United States. On March 25, 1974, Pyongyang sent an open letter to the U.S. Congress proposing direct negotiations between the two countries. Since then, it has persistently sought direct negotiations with the United States, excluding South Korean participation. It is conceivable, Kie-Pyung Oh said, that U.S.-North Korean negotiations could be productive in "opening" the North. However, as the North's first and foremost objective is to bring about a faster withdrawal of U.S. troops stationed in South Korea along with the dissolution of the UN Command, Professor Oh cautioned that such direct talks between the United States and North Korea are more likely to have grave consequences for the South. First, the talks would give the North a propaganda tool that it could use to improve its claim to being the sole legitimate government of Korea; second, it could weaken the security of the Republic of Korea by bringing about an accelerated withdrawal of U.S. troops; and third, it would add a new divisive element to U.S.-South Korean relations.

If such talks are to proceed in the future, two conditions must be met, Kie-Pyung Oh said. The first is that U.S.-North Korean negotiations should be reciprocated by the Soviet Union or China for South Korea. The second is that any negotiations between the United States and North Korea can proceed only after the present U.S.-ROK defense treaty has been recognized. When these conditions have been met, the existing defense treaties of both sides are then open to negotiation. But by no means, Kie-Pyung Oh warned, "could United States approaches to North Korea be justifiable should Washington intend to use its diplomatic maneuver vis-à-vis North Korea as a leverage against the present political status of the Republic of Korea." "This," he said, "may be counted as an act running counter to the mutual faith built thus far between the United States and the Republic of Korea."

12

CHANGING ENVIRONMENT AND THE TWO KOREAS IN THE 1980s

Seung Hwan Kim, *Research Associate, CSIS*

Strategic Environment in Asia

The strategic-military environment in Asia has undergone rapid change during the past decade. Dr. Seung Hwan Kim explained that relationships among the major Asian powers—the United States, the Soviet Union, China, and Japan—were realigned following the normalization of Sino-American relations and the conclusion of the peace and friendship treaty between China and Japan. China became no longer politically isolated and physically contained by the United States and its allies.

In the Soviet view, these developments were a strategic setback for them in Asia. What most concerned Moscow was the possibility of U.S.-Sino-Japanese strategic cooperation against the Soviet Union. Chinese collaboration with the militarily and technologically advanced United States would not only threaten the Soviet security position in Asia, but also restrict the Soviet ability to project global power. In addition, the threat of a two-front war—one in Europe and the other in Asia—would become a Soviet, in addition to U.S., concern.

These concerns, Dr. Kim believes, have had a significant impact upon Soviet policy in Asia throughout the 1970s. While calling for "confidence-building measures" in East Asia, the Moscow leadership has attempted to strengthen its strategic position around the Eurasian landmass by consolidating footholds in Vietnam, India, and Afghanistan. Soviet forces have increased drastically in numbers and sophistication. In 1982, for instance, the Soviet military structure in the region constituted about one-third of the total Soviet military force. The Pacific Fleet is now the largest of their fleets. Deploying 50–55 ground divisions along the Chinese border, the USSR has turned its attention to increasing its air and ground forces on the northern islands of Japan. Moscow also has made steady improvements in theater nuclear forces, having deployed the Backfire bomber and continuing to deploy the SS-20 intermediate range missiles.

Dr. Kim argued that Moscow's efforts have been directed toward maximizing its geopolitical strength to offset U.S.-Sino-Japanese cooperation, encircling the PRC from the West Pacific and Southeast Asia in an attempt to force China back into cooperation with the Soviet Union, and neutralizing Japan. The pattern of Soviet investment in their massive Asian defense structure over the past 15 years suggests that their aims are long term, rather than transitory. Consequently, the main thrust of Soviet Asian policy is not likely to change substantially throughout the 1980s, although economic difficulties and lagging technology may retard the growth of the Soviet military buildup.

To a large extent, U.S. policy toward Asia has been a function of its rivalry with the Soviet Union. U.S. interests in Asia have been fundamentally an extension of its global ones, which included the prevention of a disproportionate military-strategic balance in the region to deter Communist aggression and to protect U.S. and allied interests from Soviet pressure. The basic concepts of U.S. Asian policy has focused on maintaining stability with a modest commitment of U.S. forces.

Increasingly pressured by Soviet expansionist efforts, the United States determined to strengthen its military muscle in Asia in the 1980s. As part of its policy, the U.S. leadership is moving toward building up its naval forces and nuclear umbrella in the Pacific. U.S. commitments to the security of South Korea have become firmer and more credible. The U.S. efforts to create an anti-Soviet coalition with friendly nations—Japan, South Korea, and the ASEAN nations—are also an important aspect of U.S. policy in Asia. In particular, Washington continues to push for military cooperation with Japan in its defense buildup.

At the same time, Dr. Kim noted, U.S. Asian policy in the 1980s focuses upon sustaining cooperation with China to assure a Sino-Soviet adversary relationship. The continuation of the Sino-Soviet conflict diverts Soviet military resources to its borders with China and, to an extent, away from other regions resulting in an overall military balance across the entire Eurasian landmass. The U.S. attempt to develop a quasi-alliance with the PRC by offering military technology and political support, as suggested by Secretary of State Alexander Haig in Peking in June 1981, was aimed at achieving these objectives.

While both the United States and the Soviet Union are playing a China card, China's attitude is a key to the future of their relationship. Yet, the course of Chinese foreign policy is unpredictable because of internal political turmoil. The current Chinese leaders are aging, and a power realignment is likely to occur in the 1980s. Since the late 1970s, Deng and his followers—particularly Hu Yaobang (Chinese Communist Party chairman) and Zhao Ziyang (the premier)—have been the dominant faction, and future Chinese policy will depend upon the duration of this regime. This group views the opening to the non-Communist nations as a means of acquiring access to Western military technology.

Under such circumstances, Chinese foreign policy in the 1980s will be dictated by two major elements: external security and internal development. The Four Modernizations program presupposes external security, without which it becomes impossible to achieve its original objectives substantially. All evidence indicates that throughout this decade the PRC will remain a rather weak nation militarily and defensively oriented in its relations with the Soviet Union.

Korea and the Triangular Relationship

Dr. Kim pointed out that the evolution of U.S.-Sino-Soviet relations will significantly affect the strategic realities of the two Koreas. There are three possible avenues open to Beijing. First, the Chinese may substantially reconcile their differences with the Soviets, restoring close economic, technological, and strategic cooperation. This would require a substantial withdrawal of Soviet military resources from the Chinese border, the end of Soviet support for Vietnam, the withdrawal of Soviet troops from Afghanistan, and active Soviet help for the Chinese attempt to unify Taiwan. In this case, the Soviet Union and the PRC might provide logistic support to North Korea for expelling the United States from the Eurasian landmass. At the same time, Sino-Soviet competition for influence in North Korea would probably decline, and Pyongyang's relations with Moscow and Beijing would be similar to those of the 1950s. The North Koreans might well conclude that the time had come to unify the peninsula with support from the two Communist powers.

As a result, the possibility of a high-intensity conflict in Korea would increase.

Second, Peking could become increasingly dependent upon the United States, Japan, and Western Europe for rapid achievement of its modernization program and for external security, while hostile relations with the Soviet Union continue. This approach might aggravate Sino-North Korean relations and improve Chinese relations with South Korea, particularly in the fields of trade and technology and other cultural matters. This policy line is not necessarily conducive to stability in the Korean peninsula. It is likely that the Soviet Union would seek closer cooperation with North Korea by increasing logistic and military support. In the late 1970s, for instance, when the PRC concluded a peace and friendship treaty with Japan and normalized relations with the United States, the Soviets concluded a defense treaty with Vietnam and strengthened their military position in Afghanistan. If North Korea were to enjoy comparable Soviet support, it might adopt more belligerent policies.

The third option open to the Chinese leadership is to take a middle-of-the-road line, maintaining an equidistant policy vis-à-vis the Soviet Union and the United States. In this case, Peking could treat both Washington and Moscow evenhandedly by drawing away somewhat from the United States and improving relations somewhat with the Soviet Union. This option would provide greater security, substantially reduce tensions on the Sino-Soviet border, and provide independence from both Moscow and Washington.

Under this option, Dr. Kim maintained, the Korean situation would be no better than it is now. This approach requires that China push for stability on the Korean peninsula, because any major military conflict in the region would place China in a strategic dilemma: to support North Korea would threaten U.S.-PRC relations, but to abandon the North would make it totally pro-Soviet. Such a situation would make it difficult for China to pursue an even-handed policy toward the United States and the Soviet Union. Therefore, under this third option, Peking would make efforts to restrain Pyongyang's adventuristic campaign against the South. At the same time, Peking would probably be more friendly toward North Korea to break the encirclement of China by the Soviet Union and its allies, while taking a cool attitude toward the South. Lately, an increase in Chinese military and economic aid to North Korea, recent visits of Zhao Ziyang, Ho Yaobang, and Deng Xiaoping to Pyongyang, and Kim Il-sung's visit to Peking in late 1982 indicate the improved relationship between the two countries.

This relationship may not last long, however, if the Soviet Union determines to reassert its presence in North Korea. North Korea faces various economic, technological, and military difficulties, and Moscow is better able to assist North Korea than is the PRC. No matter how generous the PRC is, Peking is not quite capable of meeting the needs of North Korea either in quality or in quantity.

The Inter-Korean Relationship

In line with the changing environment in Asia, South and North Korea agreed to make a joint effort, without outside interference, to achieve reunification by peaceful means. This was announced in their joint communiqué on July 4, 1972. Efforts at dialogue continued in ensuing years, but failed. South Korea has desired a "step-by-step" approach toward greater security and gradual reintegration. To this end, Seoul has proposed a cultural and economic exchange at the first stage and political negotiation at the next.

The North, on the other hand, has demanded excessive steps to achieve immediate unification, which were reflected in Kim Il-sung's confederal theme at the Sixth Congress of the Korean Workers Party in 1980. It called for scrapping all military treaties by North and South Korea with third parties, dismantling military facilities and reducing standing armies to 100 thousand or 150 thousand on each side, and direct negotiations between Pyongyang and Washington to replace the existing armistice agreement with a peace treaty. To the South Koreans, Pyongyang's demands were too dangerous. They argued that its objective was to confuse the South and to break Seoul's ties with the United States so that the North could unify the peninsula on its own terms.

As a result of these irreconcilable positions, Dr. Kim believes, the peaceful reunification or any substantial improvement between the two Koreas seems to be unthinkable in the 1980s. In recent years, President Chun Doo Hwan's proposals for a summit with Kim Il-sung and a consultative conference for national reunification—to prepare a constitution for a united Korea and establish principles regulating relations between the two governments—were flatly rejected by the North. Furthermore, hostilities and tensions have continued to develop between the two Koreas.

The Korean Balance in the 1980s

During the past ten years, Pyongyang has undertaken a massive defense buildup, which dramatically increased the military balance on the Korean peninsula in its favor. In equipment numbers and deployments, North Korea currently has more than twice the numbers possessed by the South. The most striking development is the creation of a large commando force of approximately 100 thousand men, the 8th Special Corps, whose primary mission is to create a second front in rear areas of the South. North Korea also continues to improve its capability for inserting these commando forces by retaining more than 250 light transport aircraft (AN2s) and 100 landing craft. Quantitatively, the North is likely to enjoy an advantage throughout the 1980s because of its heavy allocation of GNP (15–20 percent) to military capabilities. Nevertheless, South Korea is expected to retain a qualitative advantage in military equipment, including aircraft and ground weapons, although it might not be sufficient to offset its quantitative disadvantage. Seoul has expanded its military modernization program in the late 1970s, which effected substantial increases in its military budget by spending 6 percent of its GNP (more than one-third of the total budget) on national defense.

In the economic and technological arenas, however, the South Korean advantage is expected to continue or even widen in this decade. Both Seoul and Pyongyang are undergoing economic difficulties, but the latter is faced with more serious problems due to heavy allocation of defense expenditures, increasing foreign debt (approximately $3 billion), and lagging technology. During the past several years, North Korean foreign trade has somewhat increased while turning to the non-Communist countries, but its total volume is still negligible in comparison with that of the South. In 1981, for instance, Seoul posted U.S. $63 billion in GNP, which was more than 3.5 times that of the North (U.S. $18 billion).

Conflict Scenarios in Korea

An important question with regard to the two Koreas is the possibility of another large-scale military confrontation in the foreseeable future. There are two schools of thought in Washington about what will happen. One school argues that conflict in Korea is highly unlikely, on the grounds that the U.S. commitment to the defense of South Korea, coupled with U.S. cooperation with China, will assure stability on the Korean peninsula. The other school anticipates a war in Korea. In this view, North Korean belligerence will not change, and antagonism among the Asian powers could encourage Kim Il-sung or his successor to take military action against the South.

It seems less likely that North Korea would attack the South while the rest of the world stands by, because under such circumstances the combined U.S.-South Korean forces might defeat the invaders. However, instability in other regions of the world could conceivably inspire a North Korean attack. For instance, in the case of a major war in the Persian Gulf, a large number of U.S. Pacific assets would be diverted. President Reagan, in fact, already established priorities for sequential operations in the event of simultaneous conflicts as well as global war, and he gives higher priority to the oil region than to the Western Pacific.

These scenarios for the alternative futures of the Korean peninsula require further reflection on the past. Should any regional crisis limit U.S. capabilities to support Seoul, Pyongyang would be likely to exploit the situation. Indeed, Pyongyang was very belligerent toward the South while the United States was deeply involved in the Vietnam war in the second half of the 1960s. For its part, the Soviet Union could also affect politics on the Korean peninsula. As in the early 1950s, Moscow might value a large-scale conflict as a means of exacerbating U.S.-Chinese relations and increasing its presence in the region through logistic and military support to the North.

In such a case, the Pyongyang leadership would be confronted with two options: all-out attack, as in 1950, or guerrilla warfare. North Korea might not seek the former option for fear of U.S. use of tactical nuclear weapons. Given current trends in the North Korean military structure, it seems likely that the North would adopt a modified guerrilla warfare by dispatching large-scale command units.

In conclusion, Dr. Kim asserted that the major factors for stability in Korea include closer strategic cooperation among the United States, Japan, and South Korea, the strengthening of U.S. military presence in the Western Pacific, and gradual improvement in Sino-American relations. However, none of these can permanently stabilize the situation unless they are accompanied by steps to ensure greater internal unity, stability, and military strength in the South.

IV

Agenda for U.S.-Korean Cooperation in the 1980s

13

ROK-U.S. MILITARY ALLIANCE IN THE 1980s

Yong-Ok Park, *National Defense College*

International Relations: Past and Present

Throughout the history of international relations, the great powers traditionally have treated the small powers as helpless pawns to be manipulated at will for their own interests and purposes. Forced to submit to the decisions made by the more powerful nations, the smaller nations were neither assured of their sovereign rights nor allowed to participate in discussions that might affect them. Over time, gradual changes have taken place so that the "legitimacy of the law of the jungle was gradually replaced by the legitimacy of the national self-determination principle," Yong-Ok Park noted.

Despite the changes that have occurred, the tendency to treat small nations as mere pawns still exists, but at least the smaller powers are now better able to preserve their independence by invoking various international laws and guarantees. The bipolarization of the world after World War II not only increased the importance of the smaller states, but it also allowed them to exploit this importance for their own purposes, occasionally through playing off one superpower against the other. In a sense, it is a form of blackmail in which the small powers could maintain the political equilibrium and gain economic concessions. As these nations constitute a sizable majority in the international community, it has therefore become increasingly difficult for the great powers to contest world affairs. By nature the small powers prefer to dilute the influence of the superpowers, Park said, by remaining uninvolved in great power politics.

Nevertheless, the small powers cannot entirely escape from the conflicts of the superpowers, if only because they depend on the bigger countries for their security. The outbreak of the Cold War made this clear. In the early part of the Cold War, the small states had to choose sides, and the choices were limited. Either they had to join the Western bloc and oppose communism or join the Eastern bloc and oppose capitalism—or choose to be a member of the nonaligned movement and be relatively free from the East-West conflict. The choices were made, Park said, reflected their own ways of preserving their security and independence. Later, as the Soviet Union and the United States began to accept their respective spheres of influence and confrontation gave way to negotiated compromises, the small nations once more found themselves in a weakened position as détente made it a much less urgent matter for the superpowers to gain the support of the small states. This was particularly true of the United States and its West European allies, who tended to belittle the strategic importance of the minor states while the Soviet Union continued to seek their support. The outcome of these two differing approaches to détente, Park declared, has been Soviet expansionism.

U.S.-Soviet Détente

World politics in the past two decades has been largely dominated by U.S.-Soviet détente. However, with the Soviet invasion of Afghanistan in December 1979, a new phase in the Cold War appears to have begun. If this is the case, then it means that the past concept of détente itself has its own defects.

Essentially, the failure of détente stems from the fact that the United States and the Soviet Union understood and applied the policy of détente in a different manner and with different objectives in mind. That is, they participated in negotiations while at the same time endeavoring to achieve their own ultimate objectives. As a result, some agreement was reached in a number of areas to arrest a crisis from escalating, to avoid a military confrontation, and to prevent a nuclear holocaust, but still each vowed to prevail over the other. It is therefore not surprising that détente could not continue.

The Soviet View of Détente. To the Soviets, Park said, "détente meant confrontation by all means to achieve their objectives while eschewing direct and total military confrontation with the United States." This did not mean that the Soviet Union abandoned its efforts to achieve military superiority over the United States, rather, it meant that the Soviet Union was employing the indirect strategy of supporting national liberation movements in the Third World to erode U.S. influence in the world political arena. Because the price of direct confrontation with the United States would be too high a price to pay for enlarging their sphere of influence, the indirect strategy pursued by the Soviet Union, Park pointed out, could be said to be one of the most effective and risk-free world revolutionary strategies in the nuclear age.

The U.S. View of Détente. In sharp contrast to the expansionist strategy of the Soviet Union, the global strategy of the United States up until the end of the 1970s tended to be one of continuing retrenchment. Throughout the 1960s and 1970s, the United States sought to consolidate détente with the Soviet Union, maintain the status quo, and achieve military parity. But events did not turn out as the United States hoped. Instead, détente allowed the Soviets to achieve military superiority over the United States and to expand their influence throughout the Third World. As a result, the United States is now faced with the dilemma of whether to allow the national liberation movements to expand freely and so give credence to the belief that capitalist forces are being encircled by the forces of socialism or discourage such Soviet-supported movements and further endanger détente. In the long term, though, the most effective means of dealing with Soviet expansionism, Park said, is for the United States to formulate its own indirect strategy and recover its military superiority.

Appeasement and Deterrence

The changing international political and strategic environment is once more causing the Korean people concern about the possibility of renewed hostilities in the Korean peninsula. Believing that wars are neither always with merit nor always preventable, the Korean people, Park said, are particularly worried about their security and about what course Korean should take in the 1980s. Shifts in U.S. policy in Northeast Asia are the source of major concern in Korea. Having learned that appeasement in the 1930s resulted in the growth of totalitarianism, the United States and its allies sought to contain the Soviet Union at the end of World War II. For this reason, NATO, SEATO, and CENTO were formed, and troops were dispatched to Korea. However, by the 1960s, the West once again appeared to seek appeasement with its enemies, despite the fact that its enemies had not wavered from their expansionist path. The same was true in the Korean peninsula. In the 1970s, the United States endeavored to bring about a settlement of the Korean conflict through diplomatic and political means and, if necessary, even by appeasement at a time when Kim Il-sung boasted that ". . . the only thing we lose in the war will be the military demarcation line and the only thing we gain will be the unification of the fatherland." In view of the determination of the North to unify the country by force, "The security problems of South Korea," Park said, "could hardly be settled by shifting its diplomatic posture."

The North Korean Threat

"The root of the Korean conflict," said Park, "has to be found in the nature of North Korea's illusionary and adventuresome unification policy." Prompted to take the offensive whenever it is militarily superior and the U.S. commitment is highly questionable, the North may well decide to launch a new attack against the South. Since the late 1960s, Pyongyang has greatly strengthened its position in both regular and irregular warfare and has achieved military superiority over the South. There is no indication that this buildup will taper off. Indeed, recent Soviet gains in the region may encourage North Korea to again undertake an adventurist policy against the South.

In the event of another war on the peninsula, South Korean forces will be faced with the possibility of isolation from the outside world. Whether or not it receives U.S. support, Park stated, is also an open question. That the U.S. decision to intervene could swing to either extreme depending on U.S. global strategic perspectives will by-and-large remain a determining factor in any future conflict in the Korean peninsula. In the long run, therefore, the security of Korea is best served by an effective military alliance system that is capable of deterring and containing North Korean threats in advance, Park said. In this way, not only is the peace and stability of South Korea assured, but also that of other countries in the region.

The New U.S. Determination

The Reagan administration's open declaration of commitment to South Korea will act as a strong deterrent to North Korean adventurist policies, Park maintained. However, he warned, any such deterrence is a positive function of the effectiveness of U.S. efforts to check Soviet expansionism. For this reason, he pointed out, "the right way of thinking is only a necessary condition for the right way of doing." Therefore, to effectively counter the Soviet threat, the United States must not only recover its military superiority, but it must also develop a counter-strategy to challenge Soviet gains in the Third World. If it does not, Park said, then regional and local deterrence in critical areas such as the Korean peninsula and the Middle East is also likely to fail. At no time, he warned, should one misjudge or discount the Communist threat, as neither the Soviet Union nor North Korea will ever be content with the preservation of a rough equilibrium.

To meet this threat, the United States must again rely on its allies rather than attempt to single-handedly deal with its adversaries. In addition, Park said, the United States urgently needs to build a chain of international cooperation, taking in the Middle East, Asia, the Pacific, and other areas. The United States cannot stand alone. Inevitably, U.S. military expenditures will be constrained by social and economic limitations. In this respect, the maintenance of a strong South Korean military force will ease U.S. commitment in the area and play a part in safeguarding peace and stability in the world. But in building a firm and stable military partnership between South Korea and the United States, Park added, emphasis must be placed on a new scheme of mutual benefits and not on the old scheme of one-sided protection or contributions by the United States.

14

U.S.-ROK SECURITY IN THE 1980s: THE U.S. ROLE

William J. Taylor, *Deputy Chief Operating Officer and Director, Political-Military Studies, CSIS*

The United States and South Korea have successfully faced a major turning point in their security relationship. The course that has been plotted is a correct one, but the two allies will still encounter some twists and turns along the way. For its part, the United States will be confronted with the problem of trying to close nuclear and conventional "windows of vulnerability" in a period of economic uncertainty and rising prices. To many, the requested $1.6 trillion for the U.S. five-year defense program is too high a sum, yet in a Pentagon study leaked to the press, the amount is $750 billion short of what is actually needed for an adequate defense. The crunch will come sooner or later, William Taylor said, when more Americans realize that there is a potential for a three-front war, that U.S. conventional military capabilities are inadequate, and that the costs of being prepared will be extremely high. The realization that U.S. policymakers have failed to make a fundamental choice between a maritime strategy, based on 15 large-carrier battle groups, and a coalition strategy, premised on modernizing and strengthening U.S. and allied conventional forces, will add to the frustration felt by many Americans. "The United States may be able to afford one or the other, but not both," Taylor warned. In U.S.-South Korean security relations, the foundation to support a coalition strategy has been laid. It may have been more accidental than purposeful, Taylor said, but the correct choice has been made.

Some Regional Considerations

Northeast Asia is a complex political matrix of superpower conflict, historic rivalries, contradictory political systems, incompatible national interests, and potentially unstable regimes. At the same time, it is an economically dynamic region with an average annual growth rate of 6 percent—one of the highest rates in the world. Understandably then, U.S. policymakers charged with the task of formulating a consistent and coherent policy toward Asia are confronted with a delicate and challenging task. "Miscalculation on basic political-military, economic, or social issues," Taylor warned, "can have the most profound consequences for the security of the United States and its allies in Northeast Asia."

U.S. Security Interests. The United States has eight major interests in Asia. Of these, three are vital and five are important to the United States. The three vital interests are to preserve the regional balance of power; to fulfill U.S. security commitments to Japan, South Korea, and Taiwan; and to have assured access to regional assets and markets. The five important interests are to dispel the belief that the United States is withdrawing from the region, to prevent a Sino-Soviet war or reconciliation, to encourage Japan to assume greater responsibility for security in the area, to maintain the security of the sea lines of communication, and to promote stability and economic growth in the region.

Asian Perspectives. Although the above-mentioned interests appear to be straightforward and clear, the firmness of the U.S. commitment to the security of the region has been questioned by many Asians. Past vacillation in U.S. policy has been the major cause of uncertainty. The statement by Dean Acheson in January 1950 that Korea lay beyond the perimeter of vital U.S. security interests and the announcement by President Carter of a phased withdrawal of U.S. troops from the Korean peninsula are cases in point.

Regional Balance: Challenges and Opportunities. The U.S. belief that the Soviet Union poses the greatest threat to peace and stability in Asia is now shared by most of the nations in Northeast Asia. A commonality of interest in checking Soviet expansionism may now be emerging among China, Japan, Korea, and the United States, but it is doubtful whether this shared concern will develop into a "community" of Northeast Asian nations. This being the case, the United States will carry out its policy of maintaining the balance of power in the region through bilateral security arrangements. This won't be easy, Taylor noted. Increasingly, the balance of power will be challenged by a continuing Soviet buildup, the economic and political dynamism of the region, and oscillations in U.S. mood between isolationism and interventionism.

Shifts in military and political forces affect the balance of power in the region, but so do economic changes. "With economic growth," Taylor said, "comes a wide range of new relationships, new challenges, and new problems." Economic growth is not necessarily always positive. In fact, economic competition among the Asian nations could adversely affect regional security. In this respect, Taylor said, six aspects of the present economic situation are cause for particular attention, if not concern. They are competition for markets and protectionism, competition for investment capital, technology and skilled manpower, security of energy supplies, protection against the effects of global recession, and the prospects for weapons development and arms transfers. To lessen the possibility of conflict arising with increased economic growth, Taylor proposed the creation of compatible (preferably complementary) market structures and consumption patterns that are in line with the products of the region.

With respect to U.S. interests in Asia, there is a need to take into account the interplay of economic, political, and military factors in coordinating U.S. policy. South Korea is a case in point. Because economic growth is crucial to South Korea's security, the United States must avoid undermining South Korea's economy while developing economic relations with China. The balance of power in the region, Taylor said, could be upset far more easily by domestic developments in South Korea than it could by conditions outside Korea. This being the case, the United States must show greater willingness to consider South Korea's priorities. In particular, U.S. policymakers, Taylor said, must be aware of the fact that democratic reforms often must be balanced against the hard realities of national security. "Over the long run," he said, "U.S. military strategy could be undermined by American insistence on transplanting American values."

Threats to South Korea's Security

Two realities underscore South Korea's security environment in the 1980s. The first is that the resolution of the Korean problem is critically important to all the major states in Northeast Asia. The second is that a solution should not be anticipated during this decade.

Succession and Security. The main threat to the security of South Korea could come from internal unrest and political instability. Having a junta on the one hand and a democratic constitution on the other, South Korea may face a period of uncertainty if and when President Chun Doo Hwan steps down in 1988. Of greater concern to the Koreans, however, is the extent to which the United States will intervene in Korean affairs.

Threats from the North. During the 1980s, the most serious challenge to the security of South Korea will come from external sources, particularly from North Korea. Believing that it missed its chance to take the South in 1960 when Syngman Rhee was overthrown by student demonstrations, the North has maintained pressure on the South through provocative action and threat of force.

During the last 25 years, North Korea has continued to improve its military forces both quantitatively and qualitatively. Allocating approximately 15–20 percent of its GNP to military spending, the North has taken steps to improve its defense capabilities as well as its ability to launch mobile offensive operations. The development of the latter, together with the fact that almost half their forces are poised near the DMZ, means that the North Koreans have the ability to strike with little or no warning.

The significant military advantage that the North has over the South should decrease toward the end of the decade. Aware of this, Kim Il-sung may attempt to gain Chinese or Soviet support by pointing out not only that North Korea will lose its military advantage in the 1980s, but also that the American people are not yet ready to support another war in Asia. It seems unlikely, however, that either the USSR or the PRC will give Kim the necessary support.

The Chinese and the Soviets. Although there may be periodic displays of movement toward détente, the fundamentals of the Sino-Soviet dispute will serve to maintain the status quo on the Korean peninsula. With neither Communist superpower willing to upset the balance for fear of being excluded, it is unlikely that Kim will obtain the assistance he requires. And this is likely to continue as long as Moscow seeks to contain China and as long as China attempts to check the Soviet Union by forming a coalition of "antihegemonist" countries. It is also possible, however, that the Soviets will abandon their policy of self-restraint toward North Korea and seek to gain greater influence in Pyongyang to disrupt Sino-U.S. relations. China, for its part, is unlikely to support an attack by the North, as it has sound economic interests in the South and a long-term need for improved relations with the United States. Given the nature of the Sino-Soviet dispute and the absence of any clear payoff to either the PRC or the USSR, it is doubtful, Taylor said, that a new Korean war will occur based on cold calculations on the part of either Communist giant.

The U.S. Role in South Korea's Security

There is a clear need to articulate a strategy for Korea that is credible both to U.S. adversaries and allies, Taylor said. To espouse a grand strategy that encompasses an entire, volatile region can undermine deterrence. Unlike the situation in the past, the United States has less room to make dramatic shifts in its Korean policy. This is because, first, U.S. security commitments are now more extensive; second, diverting units to Korea would leave divisions elsewhere undermanned in the event of a three-front war; third, the United States has no workable draft system; and fourth, it is doubtful if U.S. industry could support an extended conventional war. In the interim, Taylor said, there is the need to inform the American public that U.S. human rights ideals do not necessarily conform to the history, social traditions, or security needs of South Korea. At the same time, Americans must be made to see the role South Korea plays in supporting U.S. national security interests. And last, the United States must decide whether it will adopt the maritime strategy or the coalition strategy.

South Korea's Defense Industry

Since the end of the Korean War, U.S. troops and weapons have been used to make up for shortfalls in South Korea's forces. However, with the reductions in troops and U.S. defense spending during the 1970s, the expansion of U.S. vital security interests, and the massive buildup of Soviet and North Korean forces, South Korea under President Park moved rapidly to increase defense spending and to create the industrial base for coproduction. Carter's decision to reduce U.S. forces in South Korea was no doubt a major impetus.

Problems. The willingness of South Korea to build up its defense industry helps to reduce U.S. defense spending, but it may also create problems for the United States. First, South Korea may be gaining increasing independence from the dictates of U.S. strategy, and, second, the defense industrial base has applications in the nondefense sector that may later result in problems in trade relations between the two countries.

At home, the move to establish a defense industry less dependent on the United States is resulting in excess capacity, poor quality control, and a shortage of engineers. The fact that staff rarely report problems emerging in defense production programs, that virtually all important decisions are made by a small number of presidential advisers, and that almost all defense involvement is insured against failure through government subsidies is compounding the problem.

Gradually, South Korea is learning how to solve these problems. The United States can help by liberalizing U.S. export restrictions on defense products produced with U.S. inputs or technical data, by U.S. armed forces using Korean maintenance facilities, by purchasing military equipment produced in Korea, by encouraging private American investors to take part in various cooperative ventures, and by purchasing Korean ammunition to be stockpiled in Korea.

U.S. Role in Korea for the 1980s

With the rapid growth in South Korea's economy and defense industry, it appears that the crossover point between the military capabilities of the North and the South will be reached during the early 1990s. Of course, this is based on the assumption that events will proceed in a linear direction and that the North will not receive a quantum increase in high-technology military systems. Faced with aging jet aircraft, a shortage of manpower and trained technicians, and increasingly serious economic problems, Kim Il-sung may decide to launch an attack. Before doing so, however, he or his successor will have to assess, first, the nature of the assurances from either the Kremlin or Beijing; second, the growing capabilities of the South Korean forces; third, the nature and extent of the U.S. commitment; and fourth, the political and military situation in other parts of the world. Mindful of the determination of the North to unify the peninsula, and considering U.S. attitudes on the use of nuclear weapons, Taylor warned that the North Korean decision probably would not be negated by the ostensible U.S. nuclear deterrent.

What then is the U.S. role in Northeast Asia? There are several things the United States can do: 1) it can encourage the nations in the region, especially Japan, to assume a greater defense burden; 2) it can provide modest weapons and technology to China and assist in its modernization program; 3) it can continue to emphasize efficient integration of the industrial resources of its allies to avoid duplication and achieve economies of scale; 4) it can encourage Japan to grant concessional loans to South Korea; 5) it can continue to modernize its forces in Northeast Asia; and, finally, 6) it can assist in modernizing Taiwan's armed forces. Taylor concluded that "the general thrust of the U.S. role in Northeast Asia should be toward a strategy of coalition defense based upon strengthening formal bilateral security relations in the context of multilateral, regional understandings."

15

U.S.-KOREAN SECURITY COOPERATION: SOUTH KOREA'S SECURITY ROLE

Yu Nam Kim, *IFANS*

The Security Setting in Northeast Asia

The divided Korean peninsula has been a major source of tension in Northeast Asia for the past three decades. Throughout the 1980s, Dr. Yu Nam Kim predicted, these tensions will greatly increase as Kim Il-sung, faced with the likelihood that the South will soon surpass the North militarily as well as economically, may decide to seize the last opportunity to reunify the peninsula by force, or "at least disrupt the trend toward ever-increasing North Korean inferiority relative to the Republic of Korea."

Peace and security problems in Northeast Asia are different from those in the Middle East and Eastern Europe. As the nexus for the four major powers of the Soviet Union, China, the United States, and Japan, it is crucial to maintain the balance of power in the region. For one to assert dominance at the expense of the others could only jeopardize peace in the area. "A loss of influence by the United States," Yu Nam Kim said, "will not necessarily translate into a gain by the Soviet Union—and vice versa." This is because an individual state must take into account the reaction of the other three major powers to any attempt to disrupt the balance of power. Should the Soviets ignore this and endeavor to expand their influence in the area, then invariably they will encounter an anti-Soviet coalition.

The present instability in Northeast Asia, Dr. Kim pointed out, is the result of the continued growth of Soviet military strength in the region. In response to the apparent Soviet ambition to achieve clear, undisputed superiority, the Reagan administration has undertaken to strengthen the capabilities of U.S. forces in the area and to form a community of nations comprising U.S. allies and other friendly nations. But this still falls short of a real collective security arrangement.

In this paper, Dr. Kim contends that the U.S.-Korean security relationship plays a vital part in maintaining peace in the region by virtue of Korea's geographic position in relation to the four major powers. But, in the long run, neither South Korea nor the United States can secure peace on their own. As the future state of Northeast and Southeast Asia's security becomes increasingly fragile in the face of the Soviet presence, Kim warned, it will become necessary for nations in the area to establish mutual security arrangements. Only in this way will they be able to effectively counter the political, economic, and military threat posed by the Soviet Union, North Korea, and Vietnam.

The Soviet Challenge in the Pacific

It is the goal of the Soviet Union, Yu Nam Kim said, to achieve supremacy over the entire Pacific area by the year 2000. The drive to exploit the natural resources of Siberia, the construction of the Baikal-Amur Mainline (BAM) railroad, the growth of the Soviet Pacific Fleet, and the development of port facilities in the maritime province of the Soviet Far East all point toward an "eastward movement" from the Urals to the Pacific and raise the question of the nature of Soviet intentions in the Pacific.

BAM. The Baikal-Amur Mainline is one of the greatest railroad projects of the century. First mentioned as a practical proposal by Leonid Brezhnev in March 1974, large sections of the line have already been laid. When it is completed, it will stretch from Taishet where it connects with the Trans-Siberian Railway to Sovetskaya Gavan on the Pacific. The importance of the BAM, Kim said, cannot be overemphasized. Not only will it open up new areas of Siberia rich in natural resources, but it also will connect with the new warm water port being built at Vostochny.

Siberia. The development of Siberia is a crucial part of the Soviet plan. Comprising nearly half the territory of the USSR, Siberia has large deposits of coal, iron ore, ores of many nonferrous metals, oil, and gas, as well as an abundance of timber and water. Today, Siberia accounts for half of the explored iron ore deposits in the Soviet Union, 80 percent of the hydropower resources, 90 percent of the coal, and almost 80 percent of the timber resources. Its deposits of oil and gas amount to more than 60 percent of the Soviet Union's total. As the raw materials in the heavily populated western part of the USSR are declining, the opening up of Siberia will enable the Soviet Union to meet its needs for continued growth.

The Pacific Fleet. The Soviet goal of achieving hegemony in the Pacific by the year 2000 is apparent from the growth of its Pacific Fleet. Keeping pace with the development of Siberia and the construction of port facilities at Vostochny, the Soviet Pacific Fleet has changed from a coastal defense force to one designed to carry out blue-water missions. Today the Soviet Pacific Fleet is the second largest fleet in the Soviet navy. Its infantry strength is the largest among the Soviet fleets. Its submarine force, second only to that of the Northern Fleet, has also been increasing in numbers. And the Naval Aviation Force assigned to the Pacific Fleet includes medium-range bombers (Backfires) with antiship missiles, reconnaissance aircraft with a combat radius of 2,500 to 3,000 kilometers (2,250 miles), and more than 145 antisubmarine helicopters with a combat radius of 500 to 2,300 kilometers. Moreover, while based in the northeast flank of the Pacific, the fleet has extended itself as far as the Indian Ocean. And in recent times, Kim noted, the Soviets have been active in obtaining visitation privileges and making port calls in Fiji, Western Samoa, and Tonga in the Pacific. Commenting on the buildup of the Soviet Pacific Fleet, Kim said, "Evidence has shown on a number of occasions since 1960 in Cuba and around the Horn of Africa, for example, that the Soviets will go to almost any length, regardless of cost, to defend against any perceived threat, no matter how far from its territorial waters."

New Port Facilities. The construction of the massive port facilities at Vostochny is yet another indication of Soviet intentions to expand their influence in the Pacific region greatly. Partly in response to bottlenecks and delays that occur at Vladivostok and Nakhodka, and partly out of a desire to boost the transshipment of containers from Japan to the Soviet Union and Europe by way of Siberia, Moscow began construction of new port facilities at Vostochny. When it is completed, the port will be the deepest, most highly mechanized, and largest seaport in the Soviet Union. Already, it handles 70 thousand containers a year. By 1984, the capacity will be doubled with the completion of the second section. Over the next five years the port will get three more container terminals and automated piers for ore, grain, and coal. Before the year 2000, the port facility will be able to handle nearly 17.5 million tons of cargo annually at 64 piers. Given the present congestion at Vladivostok and Nakhodka, the new port at Vostochny will greatly facilitate the movement of goods. But at the same time, Kim warned, "Vostochny must be viewed in military terms as the largest warm water port facility for the Soviet Pacific Fleet in Asia."

Japan's Security Perceptions

Nowhere is the interrelationship between the Soviet naval buildup and its strategic expansion seen more clearly than in Japanese waters. Used to back up its expanding naval presence in the Western Pacific and to put political pressure in the Western Pacific and on Japan, Soviet vessels have been reported harassing Japanese fishermen in Hokkaido waters, sometimes within the Japanese 10-mile limit. To emphasize their point, the Soviets have held maneuvers in Japanese territorial waters by sending their ships through the Sea of Japan to Okinawa, while their aircraft have flown southward over the seas on both sides of Japan. In addition, the Soviets have carried out a military buildup on Shikotan Island, less than twelve miles off Hokkaido, and stationed troops on the Kurile islands of Etorofu and Kunashir where radar stations track the movement of Japanese and American forces.

Despite the seriousness of the threat, Japan, Yu Nam Kim said, seems to resist pressure from the United States to increase her defense spending and strengthen her cooperation with neighboring countries in defense matters. "Tokyo," Kim said, "still has not defined a defense posture and continues to pursue economic gains from the same adversary who poses a direct security threat." Employing a policy of "omnidirectional diplomacy," Japan has attempted to placate the Soviets, especially after the signing of the Sino-Japanese Peace and Friendship Treaty in 1978, by improving economic relations between the two countries. To this end, the KEIDAREN (The Federation of Economic Organizations of Japan) and the Japan-USSR Economic Committee have entered into a number of agreements with the Soviet government. Japanese loans to the USSR have also been substantial. As of October 1976, total bank loan contracts amounted to as much as $2 billion, of which $900 million was for the development and export of the natural resources of Siberia. With the announcement of the eleventh Soviet Five-Year Plan (1981–1985), Moscow is certain to press Tokyo for additional funding.

Soviet efforts to persuade the Japanese that the best security guarantee that Japan can get from the Soviet Union is an "economic détente"—plus Japanese economic self-interest—appear to influence Japanese actions. But there are also other reasons why the Japanese are reluctant to be drawn into a direct confrontation with the Soviet Union. Protected by the United States through the U.S.-Japan Security Treaty, Japan, in a sense, is one step removed from any confrontation with the USSR. As long as the U.S.-Soviet rivalry in the Pacific remains, "a strong Japanese role in the future defense of the Pacific area against the Soviet threat seems totally irrelevant to the Japanese themselves," Yu Nam Kim pointed out. In other words, the Soviet threat is perceived as something resulting from U.S.-Soviet competition and not as the outcome of Soviet-Japanese antagonism. In the same way, Kim said, the North Korean threat is considered the result of Tokyo's close political and economic relations with Pyongyang's adversary, South Korea. "This kind of threat perception," Kim said, "is bound to generate a 'free security ride' defense posture, which sympathizes with its security ally's imminent-threat perception, but which is reluctant to be involved with any countermeasures, lest the burden does not pay off."

The Role of South Korea

A Soviet specialist once argued that North Korea could become another "Afghanistan" in the 1980s, in that it could either lose its independence to the Soviet Union or become increasingly dependent on the USSR and lose its ability to conduct an independent foreign policy. Equally plausible, Yu Nam Kim contended, is that North Korea could become another "Vietnam" because it might lean toward the Soviet Union and so invite a Chinese invasion. Either scenario is possible, Yu Nam Kim said, because North Korea "occupies the heart of the strategic gateway both to the Manchuria of China and to Soviet Pacific Siberia." South Korea is also of vital strategic importance, as it serves to insulate Japan from an immediate threat. For these reasons, "a sudden change in the power equilibrium over the peninsula," Kim said, "could give rise to serious instability that no regional power would like to encounter." "In other words," he said, "both Koreas can play a substantial role either in keeping peace or to destroy it."

To safeguard the peace and stability of the Pacific region, an "All Oceans Alliance" has been proposed to counter the encroachment of "undesirable outsiders." However, unlike other security cooperation arrangements, the alliance would pursue its goals primarily through diplomacy. Such a Pacific community, Kim said, might be imperative if nations in the region are to realistically counter the "Asian Collective Security System" proposed by the Soviets in 1969 and pursued again with renewed vigor following the signing of the Sino-Japan treaty in 1978 and the normalization of relations between the United States and China in 1979. The creation of the Soviet "Asian Collective Security System," together with the development of Siberia, constitute Moscow's long-term strategy to bring about a Soviet era in the Pacific.

Up until now South Korea's role in preserving the stability of the region has been limited to playing its part in maintaining the military balance of power on the Korean peninsula. However, South Korea can assume an even greater role, Kim declared. First, a politically stable South Korea would greatly enhance the security of Northeast Asia. Second, South Korea, with its advanced economy and international economic ties, can render economic assistance to friendly nations in the region and so draw them closer to the economy of the West. And third, South Korea also can offer defense advice to those nations because it has had substantial experience in conventional and guerrilla warfare as well as in the production of arms. The exchange of personnel and ideas would form the basis of cooperation in security matters.

South Korea's defense role in East Asia and the Pacific, Kim said, is limited for technical reasons to the defense of Northeast Asia, primarily by preventing a North Korean invasion. In the event of the formation of a Pacific community, however, South Korea's role could and should expand. Present security arrangements with the United States would have to be revised both in the diplomatic and military areas. With regard to China, Sino-South Korean relations would need to be examined in view of the changing security trends in the region.

Implications for Proposals

Because North Korea continues to ignore President Chun Doo Hwan's proposal for a meeting between the highest authorities of South and North Korea, it seems very unlikely, Yu Nam Kim said, that the North will emerge from its reclusive position. Instead, it probably will join the Soviets in their expansionist plans. And there will be little that the Sino-American coalition will be able to do to check it, Kim stated. Therefore, several measures need to be taken to help curb Soviet ambitions. To begin with, Kim said, the United States should upgrade its military forces stationed in South Korea and assist in improving those of the South. Second, the United States must also provide South Korea with the ways and means of coping with Soviet expansion, in cooperation not only with the U.S. forces but also with its allied forces. Third, South Korea will need to explore areas for strategic cooperation with member states of ASEAN in order to exchange security information and military personnel and so forge a security link between the Southwest and Northeast Pacific areas. Fourth, South Korea may also want to take a positive role in developing a framework relevant to an emerging Pacific Basin Community. And, finally, security cooperation between Seoul and Washington will need to be broadened. In this regard, Dr. Kim proposed that a conference such as this one should be held each year, with the location alternating between the two capitals. This will bring together Korean and U.S. statesmen, scholars, and businessmen, to review the treaty achievements in a private capacity, to identify problems in the relationship that will need to be resolved, and to assist the Korean-U.S. Security Consultative Meeting in providing and refining an agenda for policy considerations.

16

SOUTH KOREA'S SECURITY ROLE IN THE CURRENT DECADE

Larry Niksch, *Congressional Research Service*

The development of a South Korean security role in East Asia other than for the defense of its national territory is a subject of apparently recent origins. Until the late 1970s, the attention of the South Korean government was focused on strengthening internal security and developing the economy to counter the threat from the North. Since that time, however, Seoul has initiated a more activist policy in East Asia to promote cooperation and solidarity among the non-Communist nations of the region.

There are several reasons for this, Dr. Larry Niksch suggested. First, its economic interests in the region have grown as it has become a mid-level economic power. Second, the energy crisis brought home the importance of Middle East oil, the vulnerability of the sea lanes along which oil must travel, and the viability of importing energy and raw materials from southern Asia and Australia. Third, the penetration of the Soviet Union into Asia began to threaten South Korea's access to those vital resources. And, fourth, South Korea began to doubt the reliability of the United States as an ally when the United States announced it intended to withdraw its troops from South Korea.

The extent to which South Korea develops ties with the non-Communist countries is contingent upon several internal and external factors. The most obvious are, of course, the policies and priorities of the South Korean government itself and the response of the other governments. But there are other factors. Given the economic restrictions on South Korea imposed by its limited financial and material resources, an expanded role in Asia requires a relaxation of tension on the Korean peninsula; an economic growth rate of at least 6–7 percent per annum for the remainder of the 1980s; a liberal U.S. attitude with regard to the transfer of weapons and defense-related technology, along with the granting of loans at concessional interest rates; a willingness by Japan to grant high levels of economic aid and concessionary loans to South Korea; and, last, a stabilization of world oil prices. If these conditions exist, then South Korea will be in the position of not only being able to offer base rights to the United States from which strikes on Siberia could be launched in wartime, but also the ROK could bolster the security of the ASEAN states and Taiwan and develop air and naval forces capable of effectively countering the Soviet presence in the Sea of Japan and the East China Sea.

The Expanded Role in the ASEAN Countries

Economic Support

The visit of President Chun Doo Hwan to the five countries of ASEAN in July 1981 signaled an effort by South Korea to expand its role in Southeast Asia. Up until then, South Korean economic ties with these countries were minimal, while its security role had been nonexistent after the withdrawal of its forces from Vietnam in 1973.

Trade with the ASEAN states has been insignificant. In 1978, for instance, South Korean exports to these countries accounted for less than 4 percent of total ROK exports, while its imports from the region accounted for little more than 5 percent of total imports. Of that trade, most of it was conducted with Indonesia and Malaysia. With regard to Korean private overseas investments, more than 50 percent did go into the ASEAN countries, but, again, nearly all the money invested in the 1970s was in Indonesia.

Limitations on South Korea's trade with the ASEAN states need not continue. Already, it shares a number of things in common with ASEAN: South Korea and the ASEAN countries share a common assumption that economic growth and development are essential elements in national and regional security; both the ROK and the ASEAN states have mixed economies in which the governments promote and guide the private sectors; economic policy is in the hands of Western-educated technocrats; and, also, South Korea has now reached a level of industrial development that is beginning to complement the ASEAN economies, with the exception of Singapore. Thus there exists a commonality that could provide a basis for closer economic relations, according to Dr. Niksch.

To some extent, the complementary nature of the economies of South Korea and the ASEAN states is already evident. In recent years, the ROK has signed a production-sharing agreement with Indonesia for the exploration and production of oil and natural gas in the Java Sea. With Malaysia, South Korea has shown an interest in buying a number of products, including tin, rubber, timber, palm oil, and possibly oil and natural gas.

South Korean investment in Malaysia is also increasing. Since the beginning of 1981, South Korean firms have won approval from the Malaysian government to set up a cement plant, an iron works, and a plywood mill. Other projects include building major portions of a natural gas plant in Sarawak, the construction of highways in the Kuala Lumpur area, and the building of a $233 million bridge in Penang.

Another area of Korean-Malaysian cooperation is the training of Malaysian managers and workers. To meet this need, Chungang University in Seoul has established a Southeast Asia Center for Advanced Technology Training. It offers courses in civil and electrical engineering, highway planning and construction, urban development and sanitation, and rural development. According to Dr. Niksch, Malaysia may offer a microcosm of the future South Korean economic role in ASEAN.

Despite the progress which has been made, however, there are several areas in South Korean-ASEAN relations that require a reappraisal by Seoul. First, it would appear that South Korea's initial thrust at Malaysia and Indonesia has been motivated as much by economic self-interest as by Seoul's desire to strengthen the economic resiliency of the ASEAN countries. And, second, as a result of this almost exclusive attention paid to Malaysia and Indonesia, both the Philippines and Thailand have been almost forgotten, even though the major security concerns in ASEAN focus on these two countries.

Warning of the dangers inherent in this position, Dr. Niksch pointed out that the security problems of Thailand and the Philippines have a direct bearing on the economies of these two countries, and, conversely, the state of their economies affects their political stability. A Communist insurgence in the countryside poses a threat to Thailand's ability to export agricultural products. Similarly, the Philippines is threatened by insurrection as the export prices for such key commodities as sugar, coconuts, and copper decline and affect the rural areas. "If these trends continue indefinitely," Dr. Niksch warned, "the internal situation in the Philippines could emerge as the number one security problem for the United States in East Asia by the end of this decade." In view of South Korea's growing ability to play a bigger role in the region, the ROK could assist these two countries by increasing its imports of their products and extending aid and technical assistance.

Military Support

Military assistance to the ASEAN states would benefit both South Korea and the five ASEAN countries. Possessing an increasingly sophisticated defense industry that produces a broad range of weapons, from recoilless rifles and howitzers to antitank helicopters and naval patrol craft, South Korea represents a potential future source of arms for the ASEAN states. Furthermore, given its experience in conventional warfare in Korea and counterinsurgency operations in Vietnam, South Korea is able to provide training, defense-related technology, and advice on logistics and counterinsurgency. The experience in combat, Dr. Niksch believes, would be invaluable to Thailand, while training, technology, and other advice could help the Philippines counter the threat of its own insurgency.

Several problems stand in the way of South Korea's extending substantial military assistance to ASEAN. The first is the possible reaction of China. The second is the impact of such an acceptance on the standing of Indonesia, Malaysia, and Singapore in the nonaligned movement. The third is the existence of national sensitivities in the ASEAN military establishments. In addition, South Korea is constrained from selling weapons abroad because of the military situation in Korea itself, the extent of South Korea's ability to grant credit terms to arms purchasers, and the need to first obtain the permission of the U.S. government to sell certain weapons abroad. "The future use of [U.S.] veto power," said Dr. Niksch, "will have a decided bearing on the pace of ROK arms sales to ASEAN countries." To overcome this difficulty, Dr. Niksch suggested that an agreement could be reached whereby South Korea could supply the arms and equipment to ASEAN over and above the U.S. quota.

An ROK Role in Western Pacific Defense

There are two possible defense roles for South Korea in the region. In the first, South Korea would provide the United States with sites for intermediate-range ballistic missiles to counter the buildup of Soviet SS-20s in the Far East. The second would involve the development of ROK air and naval capabilities for the defense of the

Korea-Tsushima Strait and the air space extending from Cheju Do Island southward to Taiwan. In the absence of a firm defense commitment from the Japanese government, a broader South Korean defense role would help to meet a basic goal of U.S. strategy—that is, to secure a greater allied contribution to the defense of the Northwest Pacific to give the United States more military flexibility to deal with local crises or Soviet aggression in the Persian Gulf region.

Given the restrictions placed on South Korea by economic restraints and Japan's reticence in pledging a heavier defense burden, Dr. Niksch suggested a division of responsibility among the United States, Japan, and South Korea. Under such an arrangement, the United States would assume a greater role in Asia; Japan would concentrate on defense of its home islands and antisubmarine operations 500–600 miles from its shores; and South Korea would develop its air force to provide an air screen from Cheju Do Island to the Ryukyu Islands, as well as assist in the closing of the Korea-Tsushima Strait to the Soviet navy. In the event of a war, the blockage of the strait would close one of the three passages through which Soviet naval vessels based in the Sea of Japan must traverse to deploy into the Pacific and return to base. Similarly, the establishment of an air defense screen would close one route that the Soviet Backfire bombers could use to enter the Pacific for missions against U.S. aircraft carriers bound for the Persian Gulf and against U.S. bases in the Philippines. In a real sense, South Korea's assumption of such a mission could confront the Soviets with a two-layered allied air defense system against the Backfire.

Conclusion

The emergence of South Korea as a middleman has given it economic and security interests outside the Korean Peninsula. Often these interests overlap with those of the United States, but there is no longer any certainty that the United States can protect them all. In such a case, Dr. Niksch maintained, South Korea will have to take the initiative. But whether it can or not depends ultimately on the military balance in Korea, South Korea's ability to increase defense spending, and the attitude of the United States.

17

PROSPECTS FOR BROADENING U.S.-KOREAN COOPERATION

Young Nok Koo, *Seoul National University*

The year 1982 marks the centennial of U.S.-Korea diplomatic relations. Allies for the past 30 years through the U.S.-Korea Mutual Defense Treaty and other commitments, the two countries have much in common. Yet despite shared war experiences, blood ties, and mutual defense arrangements, unwavering friendship is not guaranteed. In Korea, Professor Young Nok Koo noted, the United States was rated as the best-liked nation in a recent public opinion survey, but this was not reciprocated in a similar survey conducted in the United States. In that survey, Koo pointed out, Korea ranked twelfth, along with Thailand. There are a number of reasons for this: The first involves the issue of human rights in Korea; the second is the U.S. mass media's portrayal of the Korean government in the past; the third is Koreagate; and the fourth is the negative image of Korea generated by the popular TV program "MASH," which "evokes memories of a bitter war and loss of many American lives, . . . shows Koreans in positions of inferiority and servitude, . . . and characterizes Korea as barren, backward, and poor." Obviously, then, U.S.-Korean relations cannot be based solely on defense arrangements. In this paper, four major areas of the two nations' relationship are examined in an attempt to present suggestions for broadening the ties between the United States and South Korea. The four are: political, security, economic, and cultural relations.

Political Relations

One of the basic objectives of the United States in Korea in the postwar period was to help a non-Communist country and lay the foundations for a democratic government in Korea. But this goal was shattered by subsequent events. Following the breakdown of negotiations between the two sponsoring superpowers—the Soviet Union and the United States—Korea was divided at the 38th parallel. In large part, this occurred because the United States, having no clear goal or vital stake in Korea, was unprepared to deal effectively with the Soviets, who sought to bring Korea within their sphere of influence, and ill-equipped to cope with the decisive forces in South Korean politics.

The inauguration of Syngman Rhee as the first president of the Republic of Korea in 1948 confronted the United States with a dilemma: Should it support a dictatorship and ignore the issue of human rights, or intervene in another country's domestic affairs and risk destabilizing the regime? As Rhee pressed ahead to amend the constitution in 1952 in order to be reelected by popular vote—and then again in 1954 to lift the two-term restriction on the president—tensions mounted between the United States and South Korea.

The rise of Park Chung Hee in 1963 posed similar problems for the United States. In 1968, Park rammed through a constitutional amendment that allowed him to seek his third term in 1971. Then in November 1972, he pushed for the adoption of the Yushin Constitution that, among other things, allowed the incumbent president an indefinite term of power and almost completely unlimited executive decision-making powers and made the election process indirect. Subsequent U.S. protests, pressures, and sanctions were often received with rudeness or hostility by Korea's rulers, Koo said, and they were not necessarily effective in lessening repression or in encouraging democratic processes in Korea. To some extent, U.S. intervention perhaps had some impact on Rhee's behavior, but it had less on Park's as his government became increasingly less dependent on the United States. In fact, U.S. intervention was largely counterproductive, Koo said.

With the election of Ronald Reagan as president of the United States and the pledge by South Korean President Chun Doo Hwan to bring about a peaceful transition of power, to improve the observance of human rights in Korea, and to serve only one term, a new era of cooperation between the United States and South Korea has begun.

Security Relations

Until the enunciation of the Nixon Doctrine in 1969, Korea and the United States shared almost identical views on the security problems of the Korean peninsula. That is, both believed that not only was it necessary to contain the Soviet Union, the People's Republic of China, and North Korea militarily, but it was also essential to isolate these nations economically to bring peace and stability to Northeast Asia. Over time, however, the United States has been forced to reorient its global strategy vis-à-vis Communist countries as the political climate in the world has changed. But the situation in Korea has remained unchanged. And this, Koo said, has been the source of much misunderstanding between the United States and South Korea.

The U.S. announcement on July 5, 1970 that U.S. forces in South Korea would be reduced by one division, despite Korea's opposition to such a move, shook Korean confidence in its U.S. ally. The decision by President Carter in 1977 to begin a phased withdrawal of U.S. ground forces in the South further undermined Korean faith in the U.S. No doubt Carter's decision was colored by domestic political factors and by his concern with human rights in Korea, as well as by his initial perception of the military situation in the peninsula. Regardless of the nature and origins of the decision, however, it was interpreted in Korea as an indication of the general trend toward diminishing U.S. involvement in Asia. In particular, Korea was concerned with both the suddenness of the decision and the removal of an important deterrent to North Korea. Moreover, many Koreans feared that once U.S. forces left, they would be hesitant to return should hostilities break out again.

Faced with a wavering U.S. commitment to South Korea, Park declared in August 1975 that if the program to modernize South Korean forces was fully implemented, then U.S. ground forces would not be needed by 1980. However, Koo said, this analysis was not based on an accurate assessment of the balance of power in the Korean peninsula. Undoubtedly realizing that he was in a no-win situation—wherein he still needed U.S. support but could not completely ward off what he considered U.S. meddling in the internal affairs of Korea—President Park launched an ill-conceived public relations program to improve the image of Korea in the United States. The outcome of this was the Koreagate scandal, though no clear link between Park Tongsun and the official program of the Korean government was ever demonstrated to everyone's satisfaction. At any rate, the Koreagate affair and Carter's announcement of the phased withdrawal from South Korea marked the highest point of tension between the two allies.

The inauguration of the Fifth Republic in Korea in 1981 and the revitalization of U.S. interest in checking Soviet expansionism has been welcomed in Korea. In keeping with their pledge to preserve the security of Korea, the U.S. government has undertaken to modernize its forces in Korea with the deployment of more sophisticated aircraft as well as vastly improved early warning systems. In addition, the United States is committed to sell Korea $729 million worth of military equipment, including 36 F-16s, a "stinger" air defense system, 1,000 M-55-1 light tanks and a 34-pound antijet aircraft missile. This assistance will be supplemented with increased foreign military sales loan guarantees and military education and training grants to South Korea. At the present time, then, the security relations between the two allies appear to be a high point of genuine cooperation.

Economic Relations

Much of the credit for transforming South Korea from an agricultural society into an industrial nation must go to the United States. Providing approximately $3.53 billion in economic aid between 1953 and 1975, South Korea was able to survive a period of economic crisis and take its first step toward modernization and rapid growth. In this endeavor, credit must also be given, Koo said, to a disciplined labor force, a hard-working business community, and an articulate new breed of technocrats. As a result, Korea's GNP jumped from $2.4 billion in 1961 to $8.0 billion in 1971, to $57 billion in 1980, and $63.3 billion in 1981. Per capita GNP increased from a mere $95 per year to $1636 in 1981.

In international trade, Korea's total volume in 1981 was more than $20.9 billion. Ranking ninth among U.S. trading partners, Korea's exports to the United States in the same year were more than $5.5 billion, while its imports from the United States amounted to a little more than $6.5 billion. However, despite the favorable trading situation, disagreement over trade arose between the United States and South Korea. To reduce the level of disagreement, Korea has made efforts to increase its imports from the United States, to restrict the export of labor-intensive industrial goods, and to diversify export items. Altogether, some 40 percent of Korea's total export to the United States comes under some kind of trade restriction, Koo pointed out.

U.S. investment in Korea also has been significant. Of the 835 instances of foreign investment in Korea, 135 are American corporations that have entered into joint ventures with Korean firms. Their total capital investment amounts to approximately $310 million or 27.7 percent of total foreign investment. Korean investment in the United States by comparison, is still small. By 1980, the total amounted to about $29.3 million, or 21.6 percent of Korean business corporations' total foreign investment.

Korea's fifth economic and social development plan, unveiled in August 1981, should expand the Korean market for U.S goods and increase investment opportunities. Aiming to restructure Korea's economy to provide the economic and social conditions for a second "take-off," the projected GNP for 1991 is set at around $350 billion with a per capita income of approximately $7,700. The World Bank, Koo stated, considered this projection within the reach of Korea's economic capabilities. This being the case, Koo said, the United States can hardly ignore the present level of mutual transactions as well as the future prospects for the two nations' economic prosperity.

Cultural Relations

The early introduction of American culture to Korea was largely through American missionaries. In coming to Korea, they introduced ideas about Christian morality, set up schools, advanced the status of women, discouraged the custom of early marriage, popularized the use of the Korean alphabet, and stimulated intellectual growth through the introduction of ideas about the value of the individual. "In the long run," Koo said, "these influences were positive influences rather than negative ones."

In contrast, the influence of American popular culture introduced into Korea by American G.I.s and American movies and television programs cannot be "so uncritically evaluated," Koo declared. By dominating Korea's cultural environment, these new influences, especially as they relate to American attitudes about wealth, social distinctions, and sexual and family relationships, have "provided fertile soil for conflict in a society still very conscious of its traditional values."

Those students who have studied in the United States and returned to Korea have contributed enormously to the building of modern-day Korea. Even so, their ideals of democracy and modernization are not always in harmony with Korean traditional values. Consequently, Koreans encounter difficulties integrating the two different cultural value systems and making institutional changes to accommodate such integration, Koo said.

In recent years, Koreans have begun searching for roots in their own cultural heritage. Becoming increasingly critical of the Westernization of Korean culture, the Korean people have begun to move toward relearning such traditional Korean ideals as respect, trust, and order. Nevertheless, the disparity between urbanized Koreans and those living in the rural areas in their perceptions and behavior remains. For this reason, Koo said, "the resolution and integration of Korean urban and rural culture and/or acceptance of the same positive American values along with the preservation of Korean traditional values may be the most important and difficult task in Korea today." With regard to U.S.-South Korea relations, the Korean people themselves must work out a democratic system of government concomitant with their own cherished traditional values, while promoting understanding between the two nations through cultural exchanges. The latter is especially important, Koo warned, if the relationship is to endure.

Conclusions

To realize the best in the relationship of the two countries, Koo said, it is necessary to search out ways of supplementing and reinforcing the mutual defense arrangements and shared war experiences. As the present level and direction of economic and cultural exchanges "leave much to be desired if the two nations are to be on the best of terms," Koo suggested that the existing arrangements need to be supplemented by broader economic transactions and more diverse and meaningful cultural exchanges. "If this is successful in the future," he said, "the gap that once caused problems between two divergent cultures will be filled by a foundation of friendship and understanding."

18

WHALES AND FISHES: THE FUTURE OF U.S.-KOREAN COOPERATION

Donald Macdonald, *U.S. Department of State*

Early U.S.-Korean Relations

The future of cooperation between the United States and South Korea hinges on mutual understanding and on a certain commonality of interests. As changes in the national interests and perceptions of the two countries have occurred, adjustments in U.S.-South Korean relations have been required. This paper examines both the adjustments that have occurred in the past, and those that are required in the future.

Essentially, there are three elements in U.S. relations with South Korea: the first is economic; the second, humanitarian; and the third is security. When relations between the two countries were originally established, commercial interests were paramount. Later, as the possibilities of trade proved small, humanitarian concerns came to the fore, expressed primarily in the large American missionary presence. After World War II, the United States began to recognize the strategic importance of the Korean peninsula. With the Cold War and, later, the Korean War, the security element was brought to the forefront of U.S. national interests, where it has remained ever since.

The Three Underlying Elements

As in the past, changes in the relative importance of the three elements continue to take place. Carter's decision to withdraw U.S. troops from South Korea stemmed partly from a reassessment of the United States as a world power and also from a sharpened humanitarian concern over human rights violations and dictatorial oppression in a nation greatly aided by the United States. Notwithstanding this concern with human rights, the decision to withdraw the troops was later cancelled. Explaining this reversal of U.S. policy, Donald Macdonald stated that in part it may have been the growing U.S. economic stake in Korea, which had been encouraged by the U.S. government's desire to promote prosperity and stability. Mostly, however, it was probably the result of a reappraisal of the security threat from North Korea, now found to have more men and better armaments than previously believed. For the present, Macdonald said, the United States remains firmly committed to the defense of the Republic of Korea.

Because the United States regards the security of South Korea as an important factor maintaining peace and stability in Northeast Asia, the United States has in fact paid only lip service to the cause of Korean unification and has refused North Korean overtures at direct bilateral negotiations for a peace treaty to replace the 1953 armistice. "U.S. national interests," Macdonald noted, "have been seen as best served by ruling out normalization of relations with a separate northern regime . . . as a major reunification initiative." "The status quo, with a friendly regime guarding half the peninsula," he said, "has appeared better than the risks of change."

The economic, humanitarian, and security elements evident in U.S. policies toward South Korea are also present in ROK policies towards the United States, but they manifest themselves in very different ways because of the disparity in size, location, stage of development, as well as because of the division of the country into two hostile states. For South Korea, national security is of critical importance, given the fact that the city of Seoul, with a quarter of the total population and nearly half the economic base, is less than two minutes by jet from a hostile North Korea. Even if Korea were unified, its population of 60 million would have to be permanently and actively concerned with maintaining its security against the three vastly larger and more powerful states surrounding it. For these reasons, the United States remains, and would continue to remain, enormously important to South Korea as a country large enough to deter any attack on Korea—and distant enough not to have imperialist ambitions of its own.

The economic element is no less important to South Korea in its relations with the United States. In 1981, South Korean exports to the United States were valued at $5 billion, a quarter of its total exports for that year. In addition, U.S. equity investment stands at about $300 million about a third of total foreign equity. The balance of outstanding U.S. government loans is calculated to be around $5.5 billion.

In the humanitarian area, Korea has been on the receiving rather than the sending end with the United States ever since 1882. With relatively minor exceptions, this situation continues today. As a result, Korea can never hope to greatly influence a country with a population and wealth vastly in excess of its own.

Differences in Perception

Since 1960, Korea's rapid economic and social development had significantly narrowed the cultural and economic gap and demonstrated to informed Americans the innate Korean energy and the Korean ability to solve its own problems. At the same time, it has also given the Koreans themselves greatly enhanced self-confidence and assurance, so that they are far less disposed to seek and accept U.S. or other outside guidance. Consequently, when the United States preaches its gospel of human rights, the reception in Korea is not uncritical. This sensitivity is also apparent in the economic and security spheres. The necessary liberalization of Korean restrictions on foreign business for the benefit of the United States, in terms of residence, property ownership, taxation, and repatriation of capital and profits, Macdonald noted, offended nationalist sensitivities and domestic business interests. Similarly, the presence of U.S. troops in Korea, though requested by the Koreans, is sometimes perceived as an infringement on Korean independence and sovereignty, as well as culturally insulting. Furthermore, although the U.S. military presence is added security against North Korean attack, the same presence, Macdonald pointed out, makes meaningful reunification initiatives difficult. The North Korean demand for withdrawal of U.S. forces as a precondition for negotiation, he said, is probably not just a negotiating ploy.

Obviously, reunification of Korea is a much more important interest for the Koreans than for the United States. Korea was, after all, a unified, centralized, self-governing state for nearly 1,300 years until it was seized by the Japanese in 1905 and split at U.S. initiative between United States and Soviet occupation zones in 1945. Objectively, Macdonald stated, Korea would be better off as a unified state. Approximately half of the armed forces could be demobilized and turned to economically productive work; the national market would be greatly increased in scale; the mineral and energy resources of the North would complement the agricultural resources of the South; the full energies of the leadership could be turned to the advancement of Korea's international position; dependency upon outside powers would be lessened; and national pride and international influence would be augmented.

The problems of reunification are no less obvious. First of all, the people of North and South Korea are deeply indoctrinated in diametrically opposed ideologies and reman hostile towards each other. Second, each of the ideologies has foreign supporters who would not countenance concessions to the other, even if the domestic adherents could make such great adjustments. And, third, there are two complete power structures in being, each claiming complete sovereignty and exclusive legitimacy and either could have great difficulty yielding place and power to the other even if there were no ideological difference.

The Future of U.S.-South Korean Relations

Given the changing emphasis of the humanitarian, economic, and security elements in U.S.-South Korean relations, what then is the future of cooperation between the two countries? According to Macdonald, the element of primary concern will continue to be that of security, because the Korean confrontation remains an important part of the superpower confrontation. However, this, Macdonald warned, is a short-term view.

In the long-term, the best interests of both Korea and the United States may well be served by a broader network of Korean international relations and a lessened dependence upon the United States. With reunification, such a network would be easier to establish, as a unified Korea, less closely tied to the superpowers, could play a dynamic role in Pacific affairs and also because reunification would itself eliminate the greatest threat to regional stability.

Inevitably, steps toward reunification will bring about significant changes in U.S.-South Korean relations. This also applies to North Korea's relations with the Soviet Union. Such changes, Macdonald pointed out, would be a major gamble for both the North and the South, especially if differences between them proved insurmountable. Nevertheless, he predicted, "reunification cannot realistically be achieved so long as both halves of Korea maintain their alliances in their present form . . . yet no progress is likely to be made against domestic obstacles unless something is done on the international front."

From the U.S. perspective, any South Korean initiative directed at reunification would appear to be a major gamble which, if lost, might result in the whole Korean peninsula coming under Communist control, or in a new Korean war. The potential gain, of course, would be the relaxation of tensions within the Korean peninsula and the elimination of the costs and risks of maintaining a substantial U.S. military presence. In view of the uncertain outcome of such an initiative, U.S. policymakers would remain wary, irrespective of its long-term advantage for the Koreans. But, Macdonald warned, the United States should not be perceived as retarding what progress can be made.

Military. Inevitably, in every relationship, frictions exist between the two parties. Such is the case in U.S.-South Korean relations. With regard to the presence of U.S. troops in Korea, Macdonald noted, there will be increasing criticism of a situation in which a foreign general has operational control of most of the military establishment—particularly when that general's own force contribution is only about 5 percent of the total military manpower. On the U.S. side, there will be demands for withdrawing U.S. forces from South Korea before they automatically become embroiled in a war on the Asian mainland.

Economic. In the economic area, Korea's continuing export drive, which is crucial to fulfilling its own economic plans, will lead to growing U.S. protectionist demands. On the Korean side, there will be continuing objection to the U.S. personal and corporate business presence in Korea, especially if political instability and economic recession in Korea last indefinitely. In that case anti-U.S. sentiments among some young people will erupt into attacks on U.S. or U.S.-related business operations in Korea. The consequence might be a considerably worsened economic environment for U.S. business, and the possibility of U.S. business retrenchment.

Humanitarian. The future of U.S.-South Korean relations in the humanitarian area is less clear. The recent shift in the attitude of the U.S. public toward Korea is an example. After World War II, the United States gave unprecedented aid to Western Europe. For the most part, this support was impelled by a feeling of traditional compatibility and empathy, as much as by the fear of spreading Soviet power. Toward other and stronger regions, U.S. assistance was motivated by an urge to share its wealth and to spread the blessings of American civilization over the world and therefore make it a safer place for both Americans and the newly enlightened foreigners, as Macdonald put it. Recently, however, the United

States has grown weary of this role. Moreover, said Macdonald "the general public seems to have decided that most foreigners outside Europe are ungrateful, wasteful, corrupt, and irredeemable."

Steps to Enhance U.S.-South Korean Relations

Given the misconceptions held by both sides, there is a need to enhance mutual understanding for the sake of the alliance. Clearly, South Korea needs to be better understood by the U.S. public if the costs of cooperation between Korea and the United States—such as the maintenance of U.S. forces, or the burdens of Korean economic competition—are to be accepted along with the benefits. The development of such empathy and understanding, Macdonald said, needs to be undertaken by both sides through better education and information. In the United States, courses on Korea should be included in the American school curricula, and better news coverage of Korea should be given.

Koreans, Macdonald believes, have a much better general understanding of the international situation, including the United States, than do Americans. Nevertheless, misunderstanding of U.S. intentions remain. Commenting on this, Macdonald said:

> The Korean elite, despite the thorough exposure many of them have had to American society and education, often appear to lack thorough understanding of how American public opinion is shaped or political and foreign policy decisions made. If they do understand these things, they seem often unable or unwilling to convey this understanding to their superiors or colleagues.

In the long term, Macdonald said, Korea will benefit from acquiring a deeper understanding of the United States, whether or not the special security relationship continues. This it can do without loss of identity or self-respect. Of course, this greater understanding can never substitute for commonality of interests, but, Macdonald said, "It can greatly facilitate cooperation in areas where commonality exists, and can avoid misunderstanding and recrimination in areas of divergence."

V

Conclusions: Principal Issues and Policy Implications

19

SECURITY AND STRATEGY IN NORTHEAST ASIA: A KOREAN VIEW

Ambassador Young-Choo Kim, *Acting Chancellor, IFANS*

This year, we are celebrating the centennial of U.S.-Korean relations, and it is particularly significant at this juncture to have such a gathering in which experts of both countries seek various ways to strengthen security ties between the two nations. This two-day conference will surely make an important contribution to that purpose.

Assessment of the Regional Situation

Needless to say, the peace and stability of Northeast Asia depend largely on the changing relations of major powers in the region and the situation in the Korean peninsula. As far as Koreans are concerned, these two factors have never been separated but have been correlated in discussing the maintenance of peace and security in the region.

The security environment in Northeast Asia has been undergoing a fundamental transformation with the rapprochement between the United States and mainland China in early 1970s. This development of power realignments has moved in the direction of cooperation, in varying degrees, among the United States, Japan, and China along with the isolation of the Soviet Union from this emerging coalition.

From the perspective of the Soviet Union, the emergence of this triangular coalition inevitably means a political and military alliance against the Soviet Union. It may be for this reason that the Soviets are accelerating their military and naval buildup which had already started with the deterioration of Sino-Soviet relations in the 1960s.

Thus, the new power realignment can become a major factor in destabilizing the regional balance of power.

What is more threatening to the peace of the region is the Soviet naval expansion in the west Pacific, which has been obviously associated with and occasioned by its grand design for Siberian resource development and a simultaneous development of the eastern seaport complex. When its most important single project, the BAM railroad, connects Siberia with the eastern seaports in 1984, Soviet capacity for foreign trade and miltiary transportation will enable the USSR to become a dominant power in the western Pacific. This development may even create a situation in which the nations in the region will have to tolerate a "Soviet-dominated Pacific era" in the year 2000.

The realignment of the powers and the ensuing developments may adversely affect the effort to preserve peace on the Korean peninsula. On the one hand, the rapprochement between the United States and China has been favorably viewed, for China may be able to exert a restraining influence on North Korea's aggressive intention to unify all of Korea by force. On the other hand, the Soviet Union, feeling isolated, may attempt to destroy the emerging quasi-alliance of the United States, Japan, and China by destabilizing the status quo on the peninsula. To this end, the Soviet Union has been making a greater effort to entice North Korea into the Soviet orbit with both military and economic aid, which the Pyongyang regime has been seeking. As a result, North Korea has tilted toward Moscow, although the Pyongyang regime has maintained, in principle, equidistant relations in the Sino-Soviet rivalry. This means that if the Soviets instigate Pyongyang to initiate a military conflict in Korea, the United States and China would face a dilemma in which they would have to support their respective allies, South and North Korea, and would be unable to pursue their policy of rapprochement.

Roles of the Allies

The peace and security of Northeast Asia can be preserved and consolidated only by effectively deterring these threats, which originate either from power realignments or from North Korean aggressiveness.

The nature of relations between the United States and its allies in Northeast Asia has changed considerably in the past two decades, as the countries of the region have gained strength and the United States is not as strong as it once was in the region. In this new situation, a common defense of the interests and values shared by the allies is becoming increasingly important, so that consistent and coherent action can be established to meet any adverse trends in the region. With this policy, which some U.S. experts call "equilibrium strategy," the United States upholds its formal security commitments to its Asian allies but insists upon more equitable burden-sharing among the allies. The allies, however, may not have succeeded in creating this common ground, partly because they differ in their perception of the threat and partly because, within this framework, Japan has refused to assume its new role, which is crucial to regional peace. This state of things has resulted in what may be called "the lack of effective response on the part of the West."

The Japanese perception of the Soviet threat has much to do with the outcome of the U.S.-Soviet competition and less to do with Soviet-Japanese antagonism. The Japanese argue, therefore, that their security options must be more political than military. This seemingly comfortable Japanese position, however, involves a dilemma. The alliance with the United States is the "cornerstone" of its security policy, a factor that makes Japan an integral part of the Western world. At the same time, Japan pursues "omnidirectional diplomacy" with the purpose of maintaining complete freedom in its political and economic relations with the countries of the region.

The Soviet Union has not been satisfied with Japan's dual policy. Blaming Japan for joining an anti-Soviet bloc, just as Japan did before World War II, the Soviets have gradually increased pressure on Japan. Soviet military and naval maneuvers in the last decade in the vicinity of the Japanese waters underline this message. Unless Japan's complacent approach to its security is rectified, the security efforts of the allies in the region will eventually collapse in the face of the growing military strength of the Soviet Union.

Whatever choice Japan makes, it must be made by the Japanese people. Japan must endeavor to formulate its defense policy in line with its allies in the region. The first and foremost contribution that Japan has to make to the allies' security effort is to increase Japanese defense spending and to play an effective role in the common defense system. This policy must be implemented in the general framework of the allies' defense plan so that Japan can specialize in certain areas of defense, complementing the capabilities of the United States and other regional allies.

Japan should also take a more positive attitude in certain areas of allied defense policy. In the case of the blocking of the so-called three straits, for instance, the United States wants Japan to be able to blockade the three straits along the Japanese isles when an emergency occurs and to assume the responsibility for securing sea lanes of communication in the western Pacific. The defense of one of these straits, the Tsushima Strait, requires cooperation with South Korea. Although it is premature—or out of the bounds of consideration from the Japanese point of view—to form a regional defense organization along the lines of NATO, strategic cooperation between Seoul and Tokyo will be essential for the allies' defense policy in Northeast Asia.

Another way the Japanese can contribute will be to help their neighbors increase their national strength. Considering the constraints imposed by the Japanese constitution in security matters and the magnitude of Japan's economy, this Japanese contribution will be more conducive to the promotion of regional security. This may give rise to a old argument on how to share the security burden. The Korean position on this issue has been fairly well outlined during the recent negotiations between Seoul and Tokyo on Japanese loans, but economic aid by Japan to its allies in the region will offset, at least in part, Japan's spending on defense and, consequently, will increase Japan's overall security capabilities.

Apart from these outstanding issues confronting the allies, there is a concealed, but no less important, issue. It concerns Japan's security posture. Japan has undue influence on the formulation of the strategy of the allies in the region. The U.S. assessment of the Northeast Asian situation and consequent U.S. strategy in the past relied heavily upon the views of Japan and, therefore, unavoidably reflected, though not intentionally, the interests of Japan—directly or indirectly. Consequently, the security of other countries was a matter of secondary concern, and their views were unheeded or at least undervalued. The strategic importance of South Korea was understood only in the light of its geopolitical position in the defense of Japan from Asian continental powers. According to some, Korea unfortunately existed for Japan and not for itself.

Another area is the Sea of Japan. Its strategic importance has been neglected because Japan does not want trouble with the Soviet Union and because the U.S. Seventh Fleet, being overstretched, is unable to patrol it effectively. Thus, the Soviet Union has virtually monopolized this important area for its own purposes and made it a Soviet lake. The West must decide how to treat the Sea of Japan. Will it be like the Black Sea, completely under the control of the

Soviets, or like the Baltic Sea, which, inspite of its geographic proximity to the Soviet Union, is regarded rather as neutral ground? History shows us that the only way that Russian advances to the Mediterranean and the Middle East were stopped in the past was by the firm determination of a maritime power to stand by the country commanding the entrance of the Black Sea, with occasional demonstrations of naval strength near the area. In this connection it may be recalled that it was in the Sea of Japan that the Russians were defeated and their southward advance in the Far East was finally checked by Japan 77 years ago.

Two Koreas and the United States

Turning our attention to the South-North relations in the Korean peninsula, there are unfortunately, some tumultuous and dangerous years ahead. South Korea has overcome the political disorder and economic slowdown that followed in the wake of the assassination of President Park Chung Hee in 1979. The new republic, to establish a durable peace on the peninsula, has made various proposals to the North, including an exchange of visits between the highest authorities in the South and North for the peaceful unification of the fatherland.

For both Koreas, security and unification issues are never separate. The unification problem, although central and urgent for all Koreans, must be subordinate to security, at least for the time being, because no meaningful discussion on unification can be conducted unless both sides eliminate mistrust and both sides feel safe from the subversive activities of the other.

North Korea, however, is talking about unification before anything else, claiming that unification itself can solve all outstanding issues between the South and the North. The latest proposal for "Confederal Democratic Republic of Koryo (Korea)" is the most concrete expression of Pyongyang's thinking. It looks feasible on the surface, but it is not difficult to discern that this tricky move contains insidious traps to absorb the Republic of Korea by deception. The North's proposal also includes the conclusion of a peace treaty between North Korea and the United States and the subsequent withdrawal of U.S. troops, as well as the replacement of the present government in the South with a pro-Communist regime. These are prerequisites to the establishment of the confederal system. This is tantamount to demand for the voluntary dissolution of the Republic of Korea. This is the meaning of what the North calls "removal of obstacles in the way of dialogue." It is not surprising, therefore, that all contacts and negotiations between Seoul and Pyongyang have been totally suspended.

In this deadlocked and overstrained situation, even a minor provocative move can trigger full-scale hostilities in the peninsula. I pointed out earlier that the power realignment of Northeast Asia can be a potentially destabilizing factor for the peace of Korea. The possibility of renewed hostilities in Korea is even greater if Kim Il-sung believes that he has his last opportunity to use military force to subjugate South Korea in the face of the widening gap between the South and North in political, economic, and even military fields. There is no evidence that the Pyongyang regime after the death of Kim Il-sung would soften its aggressive policy.

Under these circumstances, the continuing presence of U.S. troops and active U.S. involvement in Northeast Asian affairs are indispensable not only for the maintenance of stability on the Korean peninsula but also for the peace of the region as a whole. The presence of U.S. troops in South Korea is, of course, to deter North Korean aggression and to act as a restraining influence on Soviet attempts to dominate the region. From a broader perspective, however, it is also to prevent the Soviet Union and China from aiding North Korea in case the North decides to attack the South. Both Communist giants are not likely to risk a direct confrontation with the United States for the sake of the Pyongyang regime. At the same time we believe that the United States should show no sign that it might waiver in its determination to prevent the use of force by North Korea or that it might comply with Pyongyang by opening a dialogue without the knowledge and participation of the Seoul government.

Apparently in some quarters of the United States there is a belief that the opening up of North Korea to the West would lead the Pyongyang regime eventually to take a more conciliatory attitude toward the South. In this view, the United States and other Western countries should broaden their contacts with North Korea—at least on unofficial levels. Actually, however, since 1973 the doors of Pyongyang opened to the outside world to a great extent, as North Korea joined world bodies including the World Health Organization and UNESCO and established diplomatic relations with many countries that already had official relations with the Seoul government. But the result was very disappointing. North Korea neither softened its militant policies to the South nor became cooperative in the matters of national unification.

In the same context, the role of South Korean forces in the security of Northeast Asia is more than maintaining a military balance in the Korean peninsula vis-á-vis the North. The Korean forces, with the cooperation of U.S. troops in Korea, can play an indirect role in restraining Soviet military maneuvers in the region. The Sino-U.S. rapprochement is not likely to have a positive influence on Pyongyang; on the contrary, North Korea has tilted toward Moscow, a factor that can undoubtedly destabilize peace on the peninsula. In view of the above, politically stable South Korea, with its enforced role in the power constellations of Northeast Asia, will greatly improve the security environment in the region.

With this elevated role, South Korea can broaden its scope of cooperation with the United States and its allies in the security of the region. Strategic cooperation between Seoul and Tokyo is essential for allied defense strategy. This may be achieved by including South Korea as an observer in the "Guideline for U.S.-Japan Defense Cooperation." South Korea may also want to participate as an observer in the RIMPAC exercise of the ANZUS and in military exercises of the Five-Power Defense Arrangement (Britain, Australia, New Zealand, Singapore, and Malaysia) to forge a security link between the southwest and northeastern Pacific areas.

Looking back over the last 100 years of U.S.-Korean relations, we cannot say that they have always been smooth and without turbulence. Shared war experiences and formal security arrangements do not guarantee unwavering friendship. To achieve the best possible relationship and to reinforce security ties, the two nations must work together not only for more economic and cultural transactions but also for the enhancement of mutually shared value systems. This kind of conference will enable us to explore the issues and problems that both countries must deal with for future cooperation. If this conference can be continued annually, alternating the location between the United States and Korea, the horizon of security cooperation may be broadened and the understanding of each other's problems can be deepened. Thus, when problems do occur, differences may be resolved with a spirit of cooperation. In this way, we can emerge from them even stronger than before.

VI

Closing Remarks

Dr. Ray S. Cline

Yesterday our distinguished Conference Chairman Jong Chan Lee started us out with some main introductory points, and I think that we can finish with some main closing points. We agree that the defense of the Republic of Korea is vital to the security of the United States and that its strength should never be second to the strength of North Korea. More generally, the allies' defensive capabilities should always be sufficient for deterring not only North Korea but all the Communist countries of Asia, which include North Korea and the Soviet Union, trying to persuade them to take a more moderate international line with less hostility, less inclination toward either threats or aggression. That is a vital strategy for our two countries.

I was glad to hear our Korean friends say what I strongly believe, that the United States still is viewed as a vital actor in the Northwest Pacific and in Northeast Asia. Later that term of reference was expanded by many to the Pacific Community and the U.S. impact through its military contacts. But, in any case, the United States has a strategic role to play in the area. We all think it is important so I don't believe that there is any disagreement among us about these basic issues. I must say they were described in detail. Difficult questions about the future that we raised were analyzed in a very sophisticated and impressive manner, and I know we will all go away feeling that we understand those issues better than when we started.

I would like to be a little more impressionistic if I may. I want to follow the example of Senator Hayakawa last night. I don't have any prepared remarks; at least, I threw away the prepared remarks I had. I want to talk to you just briefly from a personal point of view about my feeling that the 1980s are a crucial turning point in U.S. history, as well as in the history of all the free nations that have associated themselves with the United States in one way or another since the end of World War II.

In an eerie sort of way I sense that I am beginning to relive my youth. I thought that after World War II we were into a phase of building strength and alliances and economic growth that would give us security for many, many decades. It turned out to be only two decades. In the late 1960s and 1970s, as many people have said at this conference, we saw a relative decline in U.S. strength, a relative loosening of our alliance relationships, the collapse of the mutual confidence that existed between our allies and the United

States. We see today in some ways the same phenomena that I noticed in the late 1940s with respect to our relations with Western Europe. Our response then was to launch an economic, political, and military effort toward building an Atlantic community. Now, the Atlantic has many special characteristics that are not likely to be repeated or replicated in the Pacific. But I feel very strongly that the challenge of the early 1980s and mid-1980s in the Pacific is going to be the same as the challenge of the late 1940s in the Atlantic. We have to build a Pacific community to find those common threads of interest, of interdependence—a common sense of what the dangers are ahead and a common sense of the way in which we can all cooperate. The Republic of Korea provides a particularly good example for some of our other Asian friends of how they can share responsiblities as partners with the United States in making the "Era of the Pacific" a strong, prosperous, and encouraging phenomenon. I don't want to be diverted into saying what the Atlantic Community is like today, but I think we can do a little better in a Pacific Community if we exert ourselves.

I agree completely with Ambassador Kim that it is crucial to agree on the common values shared by different specific nations. U.S. security commitments should be reasonably clear, and we should all agree at least in broad terms on the kind of burden-sharing that will lead to security. Now, this is going to be an "Age of the Pacific." There are going to be security dangers. We've all remarked on the complexities of the 1980s, and I think that we can all agree that the Republic of Korea, for whatever reason, is the cork in the bottle of explosive forces in Northeast Asia, and has been that for a long time and is going to be that for a long time. As long as that cork stays in place, as long as the Republic of Korea is strong and secure with all the implications that carries—economic and political as well as military—then we can maintain those deterrent capabilities that we agree are the key to the security and survival of the United States as well as of the Republic of Korea. A reasonably manageable international situation in Northeast Asia is possible with a strong Korea holding its uniquely significant position—unique in geographic terms, unique in terms of the history of Korea as a target of aggression in the 1950s, and unique in terms of the remarkable friendship and cooperation between the United States and Korea. We can establish a kind of partnership which, if not equal in every technical aspect, nevertheless is equal in the sense of responsibility of both sides, equal in the comparative effort, and equal in the perceptions of common purpose and common values. I think we can do that.

I had an opportunity a couple of years ago to speak to President Chun Doo Hwan shortly after he came into office. He said then that his view was that our values in America and the Republic of Korea were identical, but the order of priority might be different. Korea's values, he noted, are security, stability, economic strength, and political and social justice on the democratic model. He said he felt they had to be prioritized in that order in Korea because of the dangers from the North and the mounting dangers of the 1980s worldwide, which we all have discussed here. Perhaps in the comparative security of the United States we sometimes neglect the fundamental priority of a sense of security, of a common understanding about security roles between partners that is so important to the Republic of Korea. I think communicating these ideas to one another as we Americans and Koreans are trying to do is the way to strengthen the sense of partnership.

I want to say just a few more words to you because I think that it's difficult for others to speak as frankly as I intend to. Having been a government employee for 30 years but no longer a government employee, therefore speaking for no one but myself, only a scholar at Georgetown University, I would like to say that if some of you find U.S. foreign policy and strategic policy a little obscure than I am not surprised. I think it is a little obscure, and often a little confused. So it is not you that should be worried about it, it is us. But there are reasons for it. I am very sympathetic with President Reagan's frequent remark that he inherited a ship that has been traveling for ten years in a direction that many of us think is wrong. He is trying to turn it around economically and psychologically, lifting morale, strengthening political consensus in this country, and strengthening our military capabilities. As you know, a big ship doesn't turn around fast, and the United States not only is a big ship but its system of controlling political turn-arounds is very complex and not very direct. I think the first 18 months since the election of this administration have been surprisingly and, to some, disappointingly unclear as to foreign policy objectives in many parts of the world. This seems especially true regarding Asia that, as we have joked, has not produced a good hot war in the last 18 months and therefore tends to be at the bottom of the list of priorities in Washington. I don't want to encourage you to go back and do something at the DMZ, but capturing attention is the key. Attention is often a function of troublemaking rather than constructive policy.

I do feel there is a core strategy that you will find being articulated increasingly in this city, however, and I think it will be somewhat along lines indicated at this conference. For one thing, I believe the president is finally insisting on trying to coordinate our strategic policy more than he did in the first year-and-a-half. The presence of Judge Clark at the National Security Council and the appointment of Secretary Shultz, I think, indicate a role for Presidential decision making and strategic planning that will be stronger in the second half of this administration than in the first. I can say frankly, since I'm not responsible for either the good or the bad, that I welcome the improvement and I think the performance needed improving. But I believe there is a common sense of purpose in the White House and in our government and in our National Security community along lines relative to our discussion at this conference that the Pacific is an area in which the U.S. must be a vital actor; that all of the Pacific treaty states—the non-Communist states of Asia—are natural partners if not allies. Many of them are in fact allies of the United States: Japan, the Republic of Korea, Taiwan, the Philippines, Austrialia, New Zealand—the whole Pacific rim has an astonishing set of ties with the United States. Our economic relationships in trade and commerce and our defense understandings about deterring any sizable aggression are vital matters in our strategic thinking. I believe that we will increasingly define the U.S. sense of strategic purpose in this region.

That leads me finally to my last point. It also is true that the plates of the strategic planners in this town are very full, heaped up every day, sometimes with foolish issues, but always with issues that have great urgency because of public attention. When we were arranging for the Majority Leader of our Senate, Howard Baker, to meet the parliamentarians in this delegation the other day, the congressional protocol advisers told me that there are about 150 countries with delegations in this country and that they all want to have their visitors from their home countries see important officials in Congress. Generally speaking, they had to have a rule that only heads of state and prime ministers could get in; otherwise someone like Senator Baker would have a meeting a day throughout the year just with foreign officials. This town is at the center of every headache in the world, and I invite your patience with the fact that Korea and the Pacific and Asia—despite the enormous size and importance of this region—comes low in the attention category. That does not necessarily mean low in priority. Someone has said, when the trouble comes, the attention arrives. What we should be doing is capturing attention about the long-range values and trying to get our affairs in order, our thinking straight. It doesn't involve a great many people. It involves the people that are involved in decision making, and we must get them thinking along the same lines.

That is why I find a meeting like this so encouraging. I do not feel that we have any fundamental differences of view that would prevent arrival at a high degree of understanding and cooperation as we define our Asia policies, as I think we will do more clearly in the next two years. Capturing attention for these sophisticated views is the key, however, so I conclude by saying, "Don't let what currently seems like inattention mislead you." I think there is a great affinity between the American people and the Korean people, and I think there is a great respect for Korea as a society and as a political institution. There is a great belief in the capability of the citizens of the Republic of Korea and their representatives to work with us toward common objectives that are very important.

I hope that we will continue this kind of dialogue at every opportunity, because I am sure that the way to capture attention in these difficult years is to continue rational, sane, friendly, and candid exchanges of views as we have been doing. It is a period that I cannot call peacetime; I think that we are already in a period of a war of ideas and resources, with low intensity war waged with terrorists and guerrillas. As someone pointed out, we have a much more fluid and more difficult situation to cope with in the 1980s than a simple war like World War II. We probably never will have that simple a war again. At least if we are lucky we won't, because we will deter it by skillful use of our great resources and common wisdom, to get together and cooperate in ways that will prevent hostilities. But as an oriental sage once said, "Win war without fighting the battles." That's what we ought to be doing. So I want to close by saying that is my goal. I think this conference has helped moved us in that direction. Thank you very much.

Ambassador Young-Choo Kim

I took the floor simply to convey a vote of thanks from the Korean delegates to our host and American friends. It would be rather redundant for me to say how useful and impressive this conference has been, but one point I would like to emphasize again is that our meeting at this time is not the end of our effort but the beginning of our modest approach. As I stated at the beginning of this conference, we are grateful to the hosts for these facilities, for the refreshments provided us in this meeting, and also for the kind hospitality given to the delegates individually. We enjoyed this beautiful city of

Washington immensely and enjoyed attending this conference. Thank you.

The Honorable Duwan Pong, *National Assembly*

Thank you, Mr. Chairman. I don't have any prepared statement, but want to comment briefly on this seminar. First, I want to highly commend those participants in the seminar for their great effort exerted during this two-day session, which made it quite successful, fruitful, and important. I think this seminar will be of great assistance in promoting understanding and cooperation between our two countries, particularly in the field of economics, policy, and diplomacy.

I would hope that some members of the U.S. Congress will be able to join us next year when the seminar will be held in Seoul. We have a beautiful culture and tradition to show to those congressmen who might not have had the great pleasure of visiting my country and my people, as well as my government.

Some of our national goals have not been well understood and have been somewhat misunderstood by some of the participants here. I am a former spokesman of the ruling political party in South Korea; now I have become an outspoken member of the party. I would like to make a few comments to explain why we had to start anew with the future republic, supported by the governing Democratic Justice Party, and what are those goals of the Democratic Justice Party and of our nation itself.

Mr. Chairman, I would like to say a few words about myself. It is said that Pong Duwan is the Walter Cronkite of Korea. I've been anchor man for ABC news in South Korea, but I participated personally in the new republic there because I believed that we had to start anew and show to the people that the new government is quite clean, justified, and confident. If that had been done by the old politicians with the old style and the old goals, I would never have thought of joining them. "Them" means President Chun Doo Hwan and my Party leader here, Lee Jong Chan, participating in the seminar. But we thought that this new republic and new politics were necessary for a new way of governing. What I mean is, the new kind of clean people, the great majority of people who are supporting this new path of life.

There may be a great many differences between the old regime and the new regime under the leadership of President Chun. This new government is now heading for, or aiming at, internationalizing the ideals of the people, and of the government as well. We are opening up toward a new society, or new community of the world, and everything we thought should be done democratically is moving forward. We are also aiming at a society of justice. Many people ask us why the government should be established there under the leadership of President Chun. It was greatly supported by the people. You may recall that we had serious demonstrations in the street. Look back two years ago: 70 thousand college students were demonstrating against the government, against something, in front of the city plaza. We had some economic disasters along with political instability and nobody wanted to invest with us anymore. Business leaders all around the world had been greatly discouraged by the instability they witnessed in South Korea, so that perhaps is the single reason why Americans—especially the American leadership—had come to support our new government under the leadership of President Chun. When our president was invited by your President Reagan to visit the United States last February, the two nations became closer than ever before, for we had some diplomatic mishaps under the leadership of President Park.

This kind of seminar will definitely bring our two peoples closer together than ever before for the better understanding of both sides. Those scholars and leaders in business as well as in the government can contribute greatly if they continue to have this kind of meeting, get together once here and once there in Seoul. When we hold a seminar in Korea, we would like to invite as many people as possible from all walks of life—people in the government leadership or in business or on the campuses. So please do try to invite more friends, more scholars, more leaders from every corner of your society so that we can better explain what our goals are. I'm sorry I was not prepared for this kind of statement, but I am greately honored that I had a chance to talk here. Thank you.

Appendix

2320 MASSACHUSETTS AVENUE
WASHINGTON, D.C. 20008

August 2, 1982

Dr. Ray S. Cline
CSIS, Georgetown University
1800 K Street, N.W.
Washington, D.C. 20006

Dear Dr. Cline:

    I cannot tell you how pleased I am that the conference NORTHEAST ASIA IN THE 1980s: CHALLENGE AND OPPORTUNITY proved to be such a success.

    In my opinion, and from the comments of others who attended the sessions, this conference clearly exceeded the expectations of all those involved and is perhaps the single most significant event commemorating the beginning of the second century of bilateral relations between the United States and Korea.

    If this symposium is held annually, alternating between sites in Korea and the United States, it is my firm belief that these gatherings will greatly strengthen understanding between our two peoples.

    I would like to take this opportunity to thank you for your invaluable contributions to the success of the conference and to commend the dedicated efforts of Director Robert L. Dowen and your assistant Dr. Sung Hwan Kim.

    With my best regards,

Sincerely,

Byong Hion Lew

THE INSTITUTE OF FOREIGN AFFAIRS AND NATIONAL SECURITY
MINISTRY OF FOREIGN AFFAIRS

August 20, 1982

Dear Dr. Cline :

The memory of our symposium at Washington still fresh in my mind, I would like to express my deep gratitude to you and the CSIS for the successful hosting of the meeting, which was very thoughtfully arranged under your able leadership.

Without doubt, our meeting has made a great deal of contribution to our common perception of the security situation in Northeast Asia and also to our common search for peace and freedom in the region.

I also wish to thank you for your good offices in arranging our visit to CINCPAC, Honolulu on our way back home. There we enjoyed very fruitful discussions and were able to witness the magnitude of efforts the United States Government is devoting for the maintenance of peace and stability in the West Pacific region.

Thank you again for the courtesy and hospitality which was accorded to the visiting Korean delegation during their stay in Washington.

Looking forward to seeing you in the near future,
With warmest regards,

Sincerely yours,

Young Choo Kim
(Ambassador)

Dr. Ray S. Cline,
The Center for Strategic and
International Studies
Georgetown University,
1800 K Street
Washington, D.C. 20006
U.S.A.

About the Editor

Robert L. Downen is director of Pacific Basin Studies at CSIS. He received his Master's Degree in International Affairs from the Institute for Sino-Soviet Studies at the George Washington University in Washington, D.C. and his Bachelor's Degree from Washington University in St. Louis, Missouri.

Mr. Downen served as senior foreign policy adviser and legislative aide to U.S. Senator Robert Dole for five years, from 1973 to 1979, during which time he prepared numerous legislative proposals and policy statements concerning U.S. policy toward the Asian-Pacific region. He has published several articles and monographs on U.S. relations with Asia and China, including *The Taiwan Pawn in the China Game: Congress to the Rescue* (CSIS, 1979); *Of Grave Concern: U.S.-Taiwan Relations on the Threshold of the 1980s* (CSIS, 1981); "The Reagan Policy of Strategic Cooperation with China: Implications for Asian-Pacific Stability," and "Japan's Decision to Rearm: Historical, Political, and Strategic Dimensions" (*Journal of East Asian Affairs*, Korea, 1981 and 1982); and "America's Stake in a Western Pacific Collective Security System" (1983). Mr. Downen is managing editor of the CSIS *ASIA REPORT* newsletter and has made many trips to the Pacific region in recent years.

In the centennial year of U.S.-Korean relations, distinguished scholars, legislators, and business representatives of both countries gathered in Washington to discuss prospects for continued bilateral cooperation over the coming decade. Their talks focused on joint efforts to help secure stability and prosperity in the Northeast Asian region, and on the Korean peninsula specifically, for the benefit of the Korean and American people alike. This collection of conference presentations, summarizing the most essential points of the formal papers and discussion, indicates the range of concerns and problems challenging our common interests in that region, as well as the opportunities that exist for guaranteeing future progress if proper policies are adopted. What will the deaths of Leonid Brezhnev and Kim Il-sung portend for the area's stability? Can the Japanese be relied upon to accept their equal share of regional defense responsibility? What are the policy choices for the United States that can determine peace or conflict in the years ahead? These and other questions of vital importance are discussed thoroughly and objectively in this CSIS conference report.

CENTER FOR STRATEGIC &
INTERNATIONAL STUDIES
GEORGETOWN UNIVERSITY
1800 K Street, N.W.
Suite 400
Washington, D.C. 20006
(202) 887-0200